California

Science

PEARSON

Scott
Foresman

Editorial Offices: Glenview, Illinois • Parsippany, New Jersey • New York, New York
Sales Offices: Boston, Massachusetts • Duluth, Georgia • Glenview, Illinois • Coppell,
Texas • Sacramento, California • Mesa, Arizona

Series Authors

Dr. Timothy Cooney
Professor of Earth Science and
Science Education
University of Northern Iowa (UNI)
Cedar Falls, Iowa

Dr. Jim Cummins
Professor
Department of Curriculum,
Teaching, and Learning
University of Toronto
Toronto, Canada

Dr. James Flood
Distinguished Professor of Literacy
and Language
School of Teacher Education
San Diego State University
San Diego, California

Barbara Kay Foots, M.Ed.
Science Education Consultant
Houston, Texas

Dr. M. Jenice Goldston
Associate Professor of Science
Education
Department of Elementary
Education Programs
University of Alabama
Tuscaloosa, Alabama

Dr. Shirley Gholston Key
Associate Professor of Science
Education
Instruction and Curriculum
Leadership Department
College of Education
University of Memphis
Memphis, Tennessee

Dr. Diane Lapp
Distinguished Professor of Reading
and Language Arts in Teacher
Education
San Diego State University
San Diego, California

Sheryl A. Mercier
Classroom Teacher
Dunlap Elementary School
Dunlap, California

Karen L. Ostlund, Ph. D.
UTeach Specialist
College of Natural Sciences
The University of Texas at Austin
Austin, Texas

Dr. Nancy Romance
Professor of Science Education &
Principal Investigator
NSF/IERI Science IDEAS Project
Charles E. Schmidt College of
Science
Florida Atlantic University
Boca Raton, Florida

Dr. William Tate
Chair and Professor of Education
and Applied Statistics
Department of Education
Washington University
St. Louis, Missouri

Dr. Kathryn C. Thornton
Former NASA Astronaut
Professor
School of Engineering and
Applied Science
University of Virginia
Charlottesville, Virginia

Dr. Leon Ukens
Professor Emeritus
Department of Physics,
Astronomy, and Geosciences
Towson University
Towson, Maryland

Steve Weinberg
Consultant
Connecticut Center for Advanced
Technology
East Hartford, Connecticut

ISBN: 0-328-18839-5
Copyright © 2008, Pearson Education, Inc.

5 6 7 8 9 10 V082 15 14 13 12 11 10 09 08

Pinche culo

Contributing Author

Dr. Michael P. Klentschy
Superintendent
El Centro Elementary School District
El Centro, California

Consulting Author

Dr. Olga Amaral
Chair, Division of Teacher Education
San Diego State University
Calexico, California

Science Content Consultants

Dr. Herbert Brunkhorst
Chair
Department of Science, Mathematics and Technology
College of Education
California State University, San Bernardino
San Bernardino, California

Dr. Karen Kolehmainen
Department of Physics
California State University, San Bernardino
San Bernardino, California

Dr. Stephen D. Lewis
Earth and Environmental Sciences
California State University, Fresno
Fresno, California

Content Consultants

Adena Williams Loston, Ph.D.
Chief Education Officer
Office of the Chief Education Officer

Clifford W. Houston, Ph.D.
Deputy Chief Education Officer for Education Programs
Office of the Chief Education Officer

Frank C. Owens
Senior Policy Advisor
Office of the Chief Education Officer

Deborah Brown Biggs
Manager, Education Flight Projects Office
Space Operations Mission Directorate, Education Lead

Erika G. Vick
NASA Liaison to Pearson Scott Foresman
Education Flight Projects Office

William E. Anderson
Partnership Manager for Education
Aeronautics Research Mission Directorate

Anita Krishnamurthi
Program Planning Specialist
Space Science Education and Outreach Program

Bonnie J. McClain
Chief of Education
Exploration Systems Mission Directorate

Diane Clayton, Ph.D.
Program Scientist
Earth Science Education

Deborah Rivera
Strategic Alliances Manager
Office of Public Affairs
NASA Headquarters

Douglas D. Peterson
Public Affairs Office, Astronaut Office
Office of Public Affairs
NASA Johnson Space Center

Nicole Cloutier
Public Affairs Office, Astronaut Office
Office of Public Affairs
NASA Johnson Space Center

iii

Reviewers

Elaine Chasse-DeMers
Teacher
Taylor Street School
Sacramento, California

Kevin Clevenger
Teacher
Oak Chan Elementary
Folsom, California

Kim Eddings
Teacher
Madison Elementary
Pomona, California

Joseph Frescatore
Teacher
Chavez Elementary
San Diego, California

Candace Gibbons
Teacher
Freedom Elementary
Clovis, California

Anne Higginbotham
Teacher
Arundel Elementary
San Carlos, California

Sean Higgins
Teacher
Monte Verde Elementary
San Bruno, California

Sharon Janulaw
Science Education Specialist
Sonoma County Office of
Education
Santa Rosa, California

Jeanne E. Martin
Teacher
John Gill School
Redwood City, California

Mark Allen Schultz
Teacher
Theodore Judah Elementary
Folsom, California

Corinne Schwartz
Teacher
Lincrest Elementary
Yuba City, California

Schelly T. Solko
Teacher
Loudon School
Bakersfield, California

Bobbie Stumbaugh
Teacher
Roy Cloud School
Redwood City, California

Kimberly Thiesen
Teacher
Freedom Elementary
Clovis, California

Carole Bialek Vargas
Teacher
Empire Oaks Elementary
Folsom, California

Bonita J. Walker-Davis
Teacher
Don Riggio School
Stockton, California

Debra Willsie
Teacher
Tarpey Elementary
Clovis, California

Olivia Winslow
Teacher
Earl Warren Elementary
Sacramento, California

California Science

How does energy move and change form?

What are some properties of light?

Chapter 3 • Matter

What are objects made of and how do they change?

What are ways living things survive in their environment?

Chapter 5 • Living Things in a World of Change

How does change affect the survival of living things?

CALIFORNIA Unit C Earth Sciences

What can be observed in the nighttime sky?

Chapter 7 • Patterns in the Sky

How do objects in the sky move in patterns?

Science Process Skills

Observe

A scientist investigating Death Valley, California, observes many things. When you observe, you use your senses to find out about other objects, events, or living things.

Classify

Scientists classify living things in Death Valley according to their characteristics. When you classify, you arrange or sort objects, events, or living things.

Estimate and Measure

Scientists might estimate the height of a plant in Death Valley. When they estimate, they tell how tall they think the plant has grown. Then they use tools to measure the plant.

Scientists use process skills when they investigate places or events. You will use these skills when you do the activities in this book. Which process skills might scientists use when they investigate the animals and plants of Death Valley?

Infer
During an investigation, scientists infer what they think is happening, based on what they already know.

Predict
Before they go into Death Valley, scientists tell what they think they'll find.

Make and Use Models
Scientists make and use models such as maps to help plan where to go during an investigation.

Science Process Skills

Investigate and Experiment

As scientists explore Death Valley, they investigate and experiment in order to test a hypothesis.

Form Questions and Hypotheses

Think of a statement that you can test to solve a problem or answer a question about the animals you see in Death Valley.

Identify and Control Variables

As scientists perform an experiment, they identify and control the variables so that they test only one thing at a time.

If you were a scientist, you might want to learn more about the animals in Death Valley. What questions might you have about the animals there? How would you use process skills in your investigation?

Collect Data

Scientists collect data from their observations in Death Valley. They put the data into charts or tables.

Interpret Data

Scientists use the information they collected to solve problems or answer questions.

Communicate

Scientists use words, pictures, charts, and graphs to share information about their investigation.

Using Scientific Methods for Science Inquiry

Scientists use scientific methods as they work. Scientific methods are organized ways to answer questions and solve problems. Scientific methods include the steps shown here. Scientists might not use all the steps. They might not use the steps in this order. You will use scientific methods when you do the **Full Inquiry** activity at the end of each unit. You also will use scientific methods when you do Science Fair Projects.

Ask a question.
You might have a question about something you observe.

What material is best for keeping heat in water?

State your hypothesis.
A hypothesis is a possible answer to your question.

If I wrap the jar in fake fur, then the water will stay warm the longest.

Identify and control variables.
Variables are things that can change. For a fair test, choose just one variable to change. Keep all other variables the same.

Test other materials. Put the same amount of warm water in other jars that are the same size and shape.

Test your hypothesis.
Make a plan to test your hypothesis. Collect materials and tools. Then follow your plan.

Collect and record your data.
Keep good records of what you do and find out. Use charts and pictures to help.

Interpret your data.
Organize your notes and records to make them clear. Make diagrams, charts, or graphs to help.

State your conclusion.
Your conclusion is a decision you make based on your data. Communicate what you found out. Tell whether or not your data supported your hypothesis.

Fake fur kept the water warm longest. My hypothesis received support.

Go further.
Use what you learn. Think of new questions to test or better ways to do a test.

Ask a Question

State Your Hypothesis

Identify and Control Variables

Test Your Hypothesis

Collect and Record Your Data

Interpret Your Data

State Your Conclusion

Go Further

Science Tools

Scientists use many different kinds of tools. Tools can make objects appear larger. They can help you measure volume, temperature, length, distance, and mass. Tools can help you figure out amounts and analyze your data.

You can use a **telescope** to help you see things that are very far away, such as stars and planets.

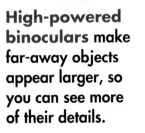

High-powered binoculars make far-away objects appear larger, so you can see more of their details.

Microscopes use several lenses to make objects appear much larger, so you can see more detail.

A **balance** like this one can be used to measure mass.

Scientists use **metric rulers** and **metersticks** to measure length and distance.

You can protect your eyes by wearing **safety goggles.**

You use a **thermometer** to measure temperature. Many thermometers have both Fahrenheit and Celsius scales. Scientists usually use only the Celsius scale.

A **graduated cylinder** or **graduated cup** can be used to measure volume, or the amount of space an object takes up.

You can use a **compass** to detect magnetic effects, such as Earth's magnetic field. A compass needle will detect and react to nearby magnets.

A **magnifier** doesn't enlarge things as much as a microscope does, but it is easier to carry.

Safety

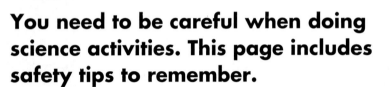

Safety in the Classroom

You need to be careful when doing science activities. This page includes safety tips to remember.

- Listen to your teacher's instructions.
- Read each activity carefully.
- Never taste or smell materials unless your teacher tells you to.
- Wear safety goggles when needed.
- Handle scissors and other equipment carefully.
- Keep your work place neat and clean.
- Clean up spills immediately.
- Tell your teacher immediately about accidents or if you see something that looks unsafe.
- Wash your hands well after every activity.
- Return all materials to their proper places.

Safety at Home

Safety Tips

- Put toys, clothing, shoes, and books away. Do not leave anything lying on the floor.
- Do not play with sharp objects, such as knives.
- Wash your hands with soap and warm water before you eat.
- Clean up all spills right away.
- Turn on a light before walking into a dark room.
- Do not run indoors or jump down stairs.

Safety

Science Safety Tips

- Think about safety tips that you follow in your classroom.
- Do science activities only when an adult is with you.
- Never taste or smell anything unless your teacher or someone in your family tells you it is okay.

Fire Safety Tips

- Never use matches or lighters.
- Never use the stove or oven without the help of an adult.
- Know two ways to get out of your home.
- Practice fire escape routes with your family.
- Get out quickly if the building you are in is on fire.
- Stop, drop, and roll if your clothing catches on fire. Do not run.

Stop

Drop

Roll

Electrical Safety Tips

- Do not touch electrical outlets. When they are not in use, cover them with safety caps.
- Always unplug appliances by pulling on the plug instead of the cord. Pulling on the cord can damage the wires.
- Have a cord that has damaged insulation replaced immediately.
- Never touch a power line with your body or any object. Stay far away from downed power lines. If you see one, call 911.
- Never touch an electrical appliance, switch, cord, plug, or outlet if you or the appliance is touching water.
- Do not use cord-operated radios or other electrical appliances near a bathtub, pool, or lake. Use battery-operated devices instead.

Earthquake Tips

- Help your family make an earthquake kit. Put water, food, a flashlight, and a radio in your kit.
- Make a plan with an adult about what to do if there is an earthquake.
- Get under or lie next to a heavy table, desk, or piece of furniture, or stand in a doorway.
- Stay away from glass doors and windows.

Metric and Customary Measurement

The metric system is the measurement system most commonly used in science. Metric units are sometimes called SI units. SI stands for International System. It is called that because these units are used around the world.

These prefixes are used in the metric system:

kilo- means *thousand*
1 kilometer equals 1,000 meters

centi- means *one-hundredth*
100 centimeters equals 1 meter

milli- means *one-thousandth*
1,000 millimeters equals 1 meter

Length and Distance
One meter is longer than 1 yard.

1 yard

1 meter

1 pound

1 kilogram

Volume
One liter is greater than 4 cups.

1 liter

1 cup

Mass
One kilogram is greater than 1 pound.

Temperature
Water freezes at 0°C or 32°F. Water boils at 100°C or 212°F.

Physical Sciences

Altamont Pass

Central California

At Altamont Pass, thousands of wind turbines capture the energy of wind. The blades of the turbines spin like pinwheels as air moves across them. The motion of the blades causes parts of a machine called a generator to turn. Inside the generator, the energy of motion is changed to electrical energy. Each turbine can produce as much as 300 kilowatts of electricity at a given time. This is enough energy to light about 3,000 light bulbs. The electricity provides power for people in Alameda County.

Find Out More

Find out more about sources of energy in California.

- **How does your community get electricity? Visit a power plant if you can. Make a presentation about what you learn.**

- **Find out how a generator works. Make a diagram showing the parts of the generator.**

- **Why do people use wind power? What problems does it cause? What problems does it solve? Find out. Then decide whether you think wind power is a good idea. Write a short report and read your report to your class.**

Altamont Pass

Chapter 1
Energy

CALIFORNIA Standards Preview

3PS1.0 Energy and matter have multiple forms and can be changed from one form to another. As a basis for understanding this concept:

3PS1.a Students know energy comes from the Sun to Earth in the form of light. Energy is a physical attribute capable of causing changes in material objects.

3PS1.b Students know sources of stored energy take many forms, such as food, fuel, and batteries.

3PS1.c Students know machines and living things convert stored energy to motion and heat.

3PS1.d Students know energy can be carried from one place to another by waves, such as water waves and sound waves, by electric current, and by moving objects.

3IE5.0 Scientific progress is made by asking meaningful questions and conducting careful investigations. As a basis for understanding this concept and addressing the content in the other three strands, students should develop their own questions and perform investigations. (Also **3IE5.a**, **3IE5.c**, **3IE5.d**, **3IE5.e**)

Standards Focus Questions

- What are sources of energy?
- What are some ways energy changes form?
- What are some ways energy moves?
- Where does electricity come from?

How does energy move and change form?

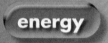
energy

stored energy

energy of motion

4 DIGITAL g

Chapter 1
Vocabulary

electricity

friction

compression wave

Explore How do machines change stored energy to motion?

Materials

wind-up toy

timer

What to Do

1 Turn the handle on the toy 2 turns. Release the handle. Use a timer to **measure** how long the toy moves.

2 Record the number of turns and how long the toy moves.

3 Repeat 3 times. Use a different number of turns each time.

You use energy turning the handle. The energy is stored in a spring in the toy. When you release the handle, the spring unwinds. The energy that was stored in it makes the toy move.

Explain Your Results

Communicate How did the number of turns affect how long the toy moved? Explain.

Process Skills

You **communicate** when you tell what you learned.

3PS1.c Students know machines and other things convert energy to motion. **3IE5.c** Use numerical data in describing and comparing objects, events, and measurements. **3IE5.e** Collect data in an investigation and analyze those data to develop a logical conclusion.

How to Read Science

Main Idea and Details

- To find the topic of a paragraph, ask who or what the paragraph is about.
- To find the **main idea** in a paragraph, ask "What is the one important idea that all the sentences tell about?"
- To find supporting **details** in a paragraph, ask "Which sentences give information that supports the main idea?"

Science Article

Heating Homes

Energy heats your home. The energy comes from fuel that is burned. Some people heat their homes with natural gas. Some people burn wood to heat their homes. Other people use electricity. The electric company burns coal to make electricity. Gas, coal, and wood are natural resources. They come from Earth.

Apply It!

You can use a graphic organizer to **communicate** the **main idea and details.** Use one like this to show the main idea and supporting details from the article.

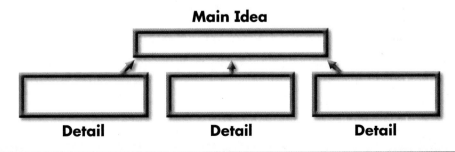

Main Idea

| Detail | Detail | Detail |

7

You Are There!

You are playing outside on a warm, sunny day. Tiny drops of sweat start rolling down your face. You decide to cool off with a frozen juice bar. Soon the treat is sliding down your hand. You look toward the bright Sun. You know that it heats the Earth. How can it melt your juice bar when it is millions of miles away?

Standards Focus 3PS1.0 Energy and matter have multiple forms and can be changed from one form to another. As a basis for understanding this concept:
3PS1.a Students know energy comes from the Sun to Earth in the form of light. Energy is a physical attribute capable of causing changes in material objects.
3PS1.b Students know sources of stored energy take many forms, such as food, fuel, and batteries.

DIGITAL

Lesson 1

What are sources of energy?

Energy moves from the Sun to Earth as light. Light energy can change form. Energy can be stored in food, fuel, and batteries. Energy can cause objects to change.

Energy

Energy is the ability to do work. You do work when you ride a bicycle, make your bed, or carry a backpack. Any time you move something, you do work. Each time you do work you use energy. Energy makes things move, stretch, or grow. Energy also causes changes in materials.

The main source of energy on Earth is the Sun. Energy from the Sun comes to Earth in the form of light. The Sun's light energy changes to heat when it strikes Earth. The heat warms Earth and the air above Earth to a temperature that supports life. Heat causes winds to blow. It makes water evaporate, forming clouds and causing rain. Plants use the Sun's light energy to make food to live and grow.

Sunlight provides energy plants need to live and grow.

1. **✓ Checkpoint** What is Earth's main source of energy?

2. ✎ **Writing in Science** **Descriptive** Write a paragraph about a time when you observed the Sun's light energy change an object.

Stored Energy

You've been playing all day, and your body is tired. You need more energy. You can't get it directly from the Sun. Instead, you get it from the stored energy in food. **Stored energy** can change into a form that can do work. The stored energy in food is released to help you move and keep your body warm.

Batteries and fuels such as gasoline and coal have stored energy too. Batteries and fuels hold the stored energy. The energy is released when you use the batteries or burn the fuel. This energy changes into useful forms, such as motion, light, and heat.

The energy stored in fuels can make a car move.

Stored energy is released when substances inside foods you eat are changed.

Wire band | Battery | Bulb

Energy Stored in Batteries

An object or substance stores a limited amount of energy. The stored energy runs out as energy is released. You can watch a flashlight to see what happens as the energy in the batteries gets used up.

Wires and batteries are inside the flashlight. The wires connect the batteries to a bulb. When the flashlight is turned on, the substance inside the batteries changes. This change releases stored energy. The energy moves from the battery through the wires to the bulb. There, the energy changes to light energy and heat energy. The bulb glows and becomes warm. The flashlight will continue to glow as long as there is energy stored in the batteries. The flashlight stops working when the stored energy is used up.

The energy stored in the flashlight's battery is changed to light energy.

As energy is changed to light, the amount of stored energy decreases. The light begins to dim.

1. ✔ **Checkpoint** What happens to stored energy that is released?

TARGET
SKILL

2. **Main Idea and Details** Read this page again. Use a graphic organizer to identify the main idea and two details that support it.

When the battery's stored energy is used up, the flashlight can no longer give off light.

Energy from Fuel

Coal, oil, natural gas, and gasoline are fuels. Each of these fuels contains stored energy. When a fuel burns, its stored energy is released. This energy changes form. It becomes heat, light, or energy of motion. Heat and light are not the same, but both are forms of energy.

An unlit match does not give off heat or light. If you strike the match, however, it bursts into flame. This happens because the tip contains stored energy. As the tip burns, stored energy changes form. It becomes heat energy and light energy.

In many homes, the energy stored in natural gas is used to cook food and keep the home warm. The fuel is burned inside a gas stove, oven, or furnace. Burning the gas changes the stored energy into heat energy. This heat energy cooks food and warms the air inside the home.

Be careful! The stored energy released when a match is lit is a source of heat.

Natural gas flows into a home through pipes. The fuel is then burned in an oven, stove, or furnace to produce heat.

These football players need energy to move down the field.

Energy from Food

Look at the young people shown on these pages. Just like you, they need energy to be strong and healthy. That energy comes from food. Your body uses the energy stored in food to grow, to stay at a certain temperature, and to work and play. Your body breaks down the food you eat into small particles. These particles are then changed to release the energy your body needs.

Your blood carries some of these food particles, for instance, to your muscles. Your muscles release the stored energy in them. Some of this energy is changed into motion, such as running or throwing. A lot of the energy becomes heat. Some of this heat keeps your body warm. Heat energy leaves your body and goes into the surrounding air.

This athlete's muscles are changing stored food energy into motion and heat energy.

✓ Lesson Review

1. Why would you eventually replace batteries in a flashlight?

2. How does the body use food?

3. **Main Idea and Details** Use a graphic organizer to state the main idea on page 12 and three details that support it.

This tarsier changes the stored energy in food into energy of motion.

This San Francisco cable car changes electrical energy into energy of motion.

Stored energy in the wound springs of this toy turns the gears that make the toy move.

What are some ways that energy changes form?

Energy can change from one form to another form. Energy of motion can be transferred from one object to another. Friction can change energy of motion into heat energy.

Changing Forms of Energy

All around you, living things and machines are changing energy from one form to another. Kittens turn energy stored in food into running, climbing, and other kinds of movement. In a space heater, electric energy is turned into heat and light. A car engine changes the energy stored in gasoline into the energy of car wheels spinning round and round. Some forms that energy can change into are listed on the next page.

Think of a dog running in the park. Moving objects have a form of energy called **energy of motion.** Moving objects, such as the dog, carry energy of motion as they move from place to place. The faster the object moves, the more energy of motion it has.

Standards Focus 3PS1.0 Energy and matter have multiple forms and can be changed from one form to another. As a basis for understanding this concept:
3PS1.c Students know machines and living things convert stored energy to motion and heat.
3PS1.d Students know energy can be carried from one place to another by waves, such as water waves and sound waves, by electric current, and by moving objects.

Forms of Energy

Chemical
This form of energy holds the particles of matter together, including the particles in food. Eating food is the way we get energy.

Motion
This is the energy of moving objects. Moving parts in machines and playground equipment have this form of energy.

Electrical
This energy can pass through wires made of special metal. This form of energy can change into forms that run appliances in homes.

Light
Energy from the Sun comes to Earth in this form. Plants make food with light energy.

Thermal
This form of energy makes particles of matter move faster. You feel this energy as heat.

1. **✔ Checkpoint** What kind of energy does a dog running in a park have?

2. **Writing in Science Narrative** Tell about riding a bike over hills and down trails. Be sure to give details about the feelings of motion you might experience.

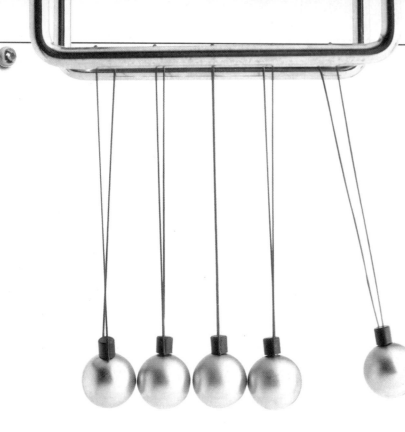

Look for Active Art animations at www.pearsonsuccessnet.com

If one ball is swung, it hits the row of balls. The ball at the other end of the row will begin to swing. If two balls are swung, they strike the row together. Two balls at the other end of the row will begin to swing. What do you think will happen if three balls are swung?

Transfer of Motion

Suppose a moving object strikes another object. Some energy of motion passes to the second object. For example, have you ever played a game of marbles? You roll one marble at other marbles lying in a circle. You try to knock them out of the circle. When your marble hits one, your marble slows down and stops. Does the energy in your marble go away? No! Some of the energy is transferred, or moves, to the other marble. Now that marble has energy of motion and rolls out of the circle. Before hitting the marble, the first marble has all the energy of motion. Afterwards, each marble has some of it. The total amount of energy does not change.

Energy of motion is about to transfer from the marble in motion to the one at rest.

Motion and Heat

When a moving object touches another object, some energy of motion changes into heat energy. What causes this change is **friction.** As objects rub against each other, each object works against the other. Their energy of motion is reduced as friction changes it into heat. This is why moving objects slow down or stop moving over time, even though the total amount of energy remains the same.

When you rub your hands together, some energy changes to heat energy.

✔ Lesson Review

1. Give examples of ways things turn energy into other forms of energy.

2. What happens when energy is transferred from a moving object to an object at rest?

3. **Writing in Science Description** Write a paragraph describing what happens when you roll one marble into another.

Friction occurs as the wheels of this race car move against the track.

Moving a loose rope from side to side on a table makes energy move forward along the rope in the form of waves.

Lesson 3

What are some ways energy moves?

Waves carry energy from one place to another. Water waves carry energy forward as water moves in place. Sound waves carry energy forward as air particles move in place. Earthquake waves carry energy forward as the ground moves in place.

Water Waves

CRASH! Ocean waves splash onto the beach. Clearly, these waves carry plenty of energy!

If you could look at a water wave from the side, it would look much like the moving rope above. Notice that parts of the rope take turns going from side to side. Energy causes this effect as it travels from one end of the rope to the other. The rope itself does not travel forward.

Water waves can be as small as the ripples in a bucket of water. Waves that hurricanes cause can be huge. How big the wave is depends on how much energy it carries. Swimmers feel the energy of water waves when they float in the ocean. The waves move them up and down and back and forth. They stay in about the same position they were in before the wave came by.

Ocean waves carry energy.

Standards Focus **3PS1.0** Energy and matter have multiple forms and can be changed from one form to another. As a basis for understanding this concept:
3PS1.d Students know energy can be carried from one place to another by waves, such as water waves and sound waves, by electric current, and by moving objects.

18

Small balls in a tub can show
how waves transfer energy.

Making Waves

A tub with water and several balls can
show how water waves transfer energy.
If one end of the tub is lifted a little and
then put down, a wave spreads through
the water. As the wave moves past the
balls, the balls bob up and then down.
They may even move back and forth
a little, but they don't move from one
place to another. They stay in the same
location they were in before the tub was
lifted. Energy travels through the water
to the end of the tub. The balls show how
the water itself does not travel forward.

A wave lifts the first
ball as the wave moves
from left to right.

The first ball drops
back down. The wave
lifts a second ball.

1. ✓**Checkpoint** What determines the
   size of a water wave?

2. ✏️**Writing in Science** **Narrative** Write a
   story about a swim in the ocean. Be sure to
   explain the effect of the ocean's waves on
   the person's body.

The second ball drops
back down. Another
wave moving through
the water lifts the first
ball again.

Sound Waves

The energy of back-and-forth vibrations in matter makes sound. Think about the sound of a bell, for example. As the bell rings, its vibrations push air particles together. Then the air particles spread apart. This back-and-forth movement of particles is called a **compression wave.** Sound waves are compression waves.

Look at the picture below. Sound waves carry energy through air like the compressions that move along a coiled spring. A sound wave travels as air particles are pushed together and then move apart. The particles themselves do not move along with the sound wave. They just move forward and then back.

Transfer of Sound Energy

Sound can create vibrations in distant objects. Think of listening to a saxophone. Sound waves travel from the instrument to your ear. When sound waves strike your eardrum, they cause it to vibrate. Sound energy has traveled from its source to your ear without the two objects coming into contact.

Find the places where the coils in the spring are pushed together. Find the places where the coils are spread apart. Sound waves carry energy from one place to another in this way.

Playing a saxophone causes its parts to vibrate. The vibrations make sound.

Hearing Sound

The eardrum is a thin, skin-like layer stretched across the inside of the ear. Vibrations of the eardrum travel along bones to other parts inside the ear. A signal travels from there to the brain. Your brain helps you to understand the sound and where it came from.

Sound is carried in compression waves. Sound waves reach the ear and cause parts to vibrate.

Eardrum

1. **✓ Checkpoint** What happens when you hear a sound?

2. **Main Idea and Details** Write a summary of the main idea and supporting details for the section Sound Waves on page 20.

Earthquakes

Have you ever built a house out of playing cards? It doesn't take much to knock it over. A sudden bump makes vibrations that send waves. The waves cause the house to shake apart. In a similar way, parts of Earth's crust can shift suddenly. These shifts send energy carried by waves in all directions. The energy causes the ground to vibrate. Buildings may fall down. The ground may crack, and roads may fall apart. It's an earthquake!

The Loma Prieta earthquake in 1989 damaged this road in Oakland, California.

Earthquake Waves

Earthquakes actually cause three kinds of waves. Some of the energy travels in waves like sound waves. They push the ground in the direction they are traveling. The ground then moves back. Energy also travels in waves like those on the surface of water. They shake the ground up and down. The rest of the energy sends waves that shake the ground from side to side.

The most energy in earthquake waves is where the earthquake happens. Buildings and roads there receive the most damage. As the waves travel farther from the starting point, they lose strength. Strong earthquakes, though, can be felt hundreds of kilometers away.

Waves of energy from an earthquake cause cracks like this one.

✓ Lesson Review

1. What are some waves that carry energy?

2. How are waves that earthquakes cause like waves that travel through water? How are they like sound waves that travel through air?

TARGET SKILL 3. **Main Idea and Details** Give the main idea for what you have learned about earthquake waves. List details to support your answer.

Parts of this parking garage snapped during a 1994 earthquake.

Where does electricity come from?

Electrical energy has a source. It is carried through wires to other places. Electrical energy is changed to more familiar forms of energy, such as heat, light, and motion.

Electrical Energy

Power plants use fuels, water, wind, or nuclear power to generate electrical energy. Then it moves as electricity from the power plant through wires to your home. **Electricity** is a form of energy that can flow as a charge through a wire. Once in your home, electricity is changed into other forms of energy, such as heat, light, and motion.

Power Source
Electrical energy is produced in a power station.

Standards Focus 3PS1.0 Energy and matter have multiple forms and can be changed from one form to another. As a basis for understanding this concept: **3PS1.d** Students know energy can be carried from one place to another by waves, such as water waves and sound waves, by electric current, and by moving objects.

Now you can open the refrigerator and get a snack. You can then turn on the light in your room, plop in a CD, and turn up the sound. Electricity is the energy that turns on the many things you use every day.

1. **✓ Checkpoint** Name three uses of electrical energy inside your home and tell how the energy is changed.

2. **✏ Writing in Science Formal letter** In a letter to your power company, ask how electricity is safely sent to your home.

Transmission Wires
The electrical energy is carried by electric current through wires. The wires connect the power station to where electricity will be used in homes and businesses.

Power Destination
Electricity flows through wires to electrical outlets inside buildings. When a plug is put into an outlet, the electricity flows into the object at the end of the plug.

Electrical energy removes heat and is changed into light in this refrigerator.

Sources of Electricity

Has your home ever had a power failure? If so, you may have realized just how many things run on electricity. Television sets, computers, lamps, refrigerators, washing machines, and hair dryers don't work without electricity. Each of these appliances changes electrical energy into another form of energy that people can use.

Electrical energy is produced in power plants from turbines that spin. Different sources of energy spin the turbines. The energy may come from moving water. It may come from the heat from burning coal. It may come from the heat that special fuel in nuclear reactors produces. Even the energy in sunlight and wind is used to produce electrical energy. Electrical energy may be only one form of energy, but, for us, it's very useful.

✓ Lesson Review

1. List five ways to change energy into electricity.

2. How is electrical energy moved from one place to another?

3. **Writing in Science Narrative** Write a story about a day without electricity. Be sure to name the appliances you cannot use without a source of electrical energy.

A Bay Area Rapid Transit train moves through Oakland, California. Electrical energy is changed into energy of motion and heat.

At this plant in Moss Landing, California, natural gas is burned to produce heat energy. The heat is then changed into electricity.

The energy of moving water is used to produce electricity at this power station on the Sacramento River in California.

These windmills on Altamont Pass near Livermore, California, change wind energy into electricity.

Nuclear energy is used to produce heat that is turned into electricity at this power station near San Luis Obispo, California.

Measuring Temperature

Recording temperature is one way to measure heat. You can use different scales to measure temperature.

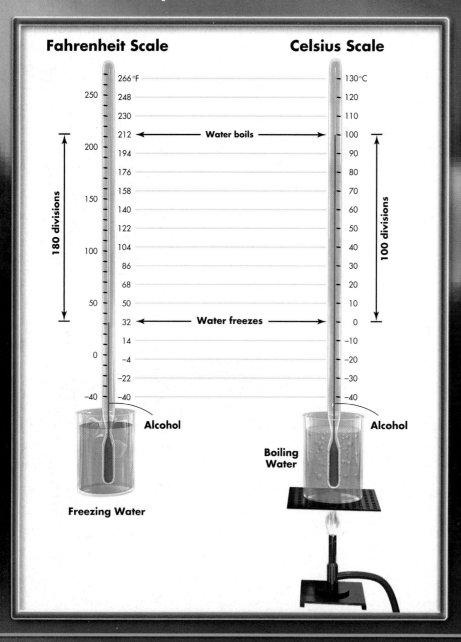

Fahrenheit Scale

Celsius Scale

266°F · 130°C
250 · 248 · 120
230 · 110
212 ← Water boils → 100
200 · 194 · 90
176 · 80
158 · 70
150 · 140 · 60
122 · 50
100 · 104 · 40
86 · 30
68 · 20
50 · 50 · 10
32 ← Water freezes → 0
14 · −10
0 · −4 · −20
−22 · −30
−40 · −40 · −40

180 divisions

100 divisions

Alcohol

Alcohol

Freezing Water

Boiling Water

The Celsius scale is often used in science. The Fahrenheit scale is often used in everyday life, such as reading the temperature outdoors. Sometimes both scales are used.

Degrees Celsius is written °C. So 40°C is read "forty degrees Celsius."

Degrees Fahrenheit is written °F. So 40°F is read "forty degrees Fahrenheit."

 What is the boiling point of water on the Celsius scale? What is the boiling point on the Fahrenheit scale?

 What is the freezing point of water on the Celsius scale? What is the freezing point of water on the Fahrenheit scale?

 About what is the temperature in degrees Fahrenheit when it is 30°C?

Lab zone Take-Home Activity

Watch the weather report on TV. Are temperatures given in degrees Fahrenheit, Celsius, or both? Make a list of three cities talked about in the report. Write down their temperatures in degrees Fahrenheit and in degrees Celsius. You can use the thermometers shown here.

Investigate How can you observe the effects of energy carried by sound?

Materials

safety goggles

cup

plastic wrap

rubber band

salt

metric ruler

What to Do

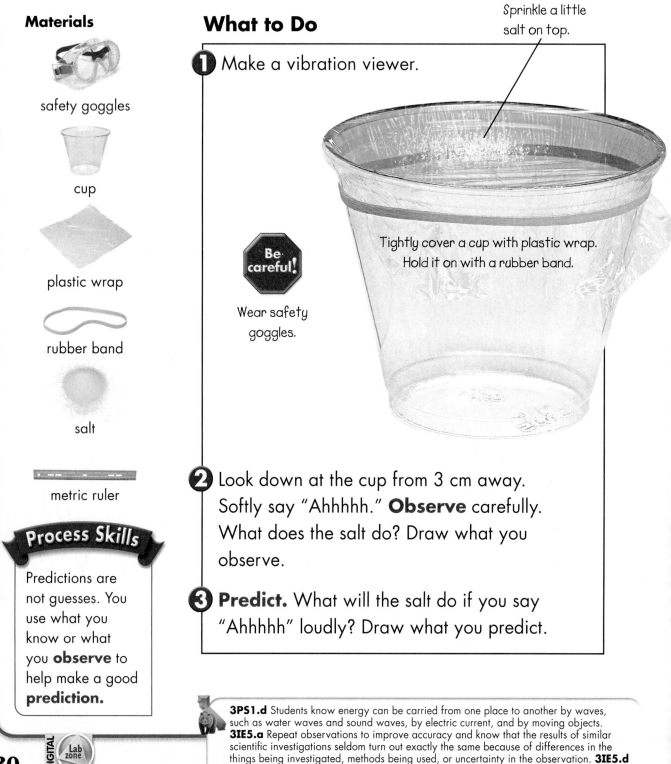

Sprinkle a little salt on top.

1 Make a vibration viewer.

Be careful!

Wear safety goggles.

Tightly cover a cup with plastic wrap. Hold it on with a rubber band.

2 Look down at the cup from 3 cm away. Softly say "Ahhhhh." **Observe** carefully. What does the salt do? Draw what you observe.

3 **Predict.** What will the salt do if you say "Ahhhhh" loudly? Draw what you predict.

3PS1.d Students know energy can be carried from one place to another by waves, such as water waves and sound waves, by electric current, and by moving objects. **3IE5.a** Repeat observations to improve accuracy and know that the results of similar scientific investigations seldom turn out exactly the same because of differences in the things being investigated, methods being used, or uncertainty in the observation. **3IE5.d** Predict the outcome of a simple investigation and compare the result with the prediction.

④ Test your prediction. Draw what you observe.

⑤ Repeat. Are your results exactly the same each time?

Observation	Prediction	Observation
Saying "Ahhhhh" Softly	Saying "Ahhhhh" Loudly	Saying "Ahhhhh" Loudly

Explain Your Results

1. Compare your result with your **prediction.**

2. How did your **observations** provide evidence that sound waves can carry energy? Explain.

Go Further

What effect does distance have on the energy sound waves carry? Design an investigation to answer this question. Describe and show how to perform it safely.

Chapter 1 Reviewing Key Concepts

Focus on the BIG Idea

Machines and living things convert stored energy into motion and heat. Each form of energy can change into another form. Waves, moving objects, and electric current carry energy.

Lesson 1

What are sources of energy?
- Energy is the ability to do work. Energy makes things move, stretch, or grow. Energy causes changes in objects.
- Energy comes from the Sun to Earth in the form of light.
- Stored energy takes many forms, such as food, fuel, and batteries.

Lesson 2

What are some ways that energy changes form?
- Energy can change from one form to another.
- Machines and living things change stored energy to the energy of motion and heat.
- Energy of motion can be transferred when a moving object strikes another object.
- Friction changes energy of motion into heat energy.

Lesson 3

What are some ways energy moves?
- Energy is carried from one place to another by waves in water.
- Energy is carried from one place to another by sound waves.
- Energy is carried from one place to another by waves from earthquakes.

Lesson 4

Where does electricity come from?
- Electrical energy comes from power plants.
- Electrical energy travels through wires as current.
- Electrical energy is changed to more useful forms of energy, such as heat, light, and motion.

Cross-Curricular Links

English–Language Arts

Building Vocabulary

Look again at page 4. Look at the picture behind the word *energy*. Write a paragraph explaining how the picture represents the word. Then describe another picture that could be used to represent *energy*.

Mathematics

Food Energy

Stored energy in food is measured in Calories. Jon gets 2,000 Calories of energy from food each day. How much energy does he get in a week?

Challenge!

History–Social Studies

Generating Electricity

Use the library-media center to find out which natural resources your community uses to generate electricity. Create a poster showing what you learn.

English–Language Arts

Making Waves

Make waves in a plastic tub, using water and some floating objects. Write about what you observed and what you learned. Follow steps to organize your information before you write.

Chapter 1 Review/Test

Use Vocabulary

compression wave (page 20)	**energy of motion** (page 14)
electricity (page 24)	**friction** (page 17)
stored energy (page 9)	**energy** (page 10)

Fill in the blanks with the correct term. If you have trouble answering a question, read the listed page again.

1. Electrical energy that moves through wires is _____.

2. A(n) _____ squeezes particles together, which then spread apart.

3. _____ is the ability to do work.

4. Every moving object has _____.

5. _____ changes energy of motion into heat.

6. Energy in food, fuel, and batteries that can be released to create motion, light, and heat is _____.

Think About It

7. In what ways does the Sun's energy affect Earth?

8. How are the Sun, a campfire, and a street lamp alike?

9. How can you increase your energy of motion while riding a bicycle?

10. How do waves cause a swimmer to bob up and down?

11. **Process Skills** **Interpret Data** The bar graph shows data for three kinds of batteries. Use it to order the batteries from least to greatest amount of stored energy.

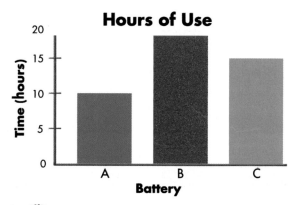

Hours of Use

12. **TARGET SKILL** **Main Idea and Details** Use the graphic organizer below. Fill in details that support the main idea.

Energy has many forms.

13. **Writing in Science**
Description Describe what happens when you kick a soccer ball. Use the terms *stored energy, energy of motion, transfer of motion,* and *friction.*

California Standards Practice

Write the letter of the correct answer.

14. What form of energy comes from the Sun?
   A heat
   B light
   C fuel
   D stored energy

15. Which is a form of stored energy?
   A heat
   B light
   C fuel
   D motion

16. What kind of energy changes to light in a bulb?
   A electrical energy
   B energy of motion
   C heat energy
   D light energy

17. Which of these forms of energy can damage buildings when an earthquake occurs?
   A light
   B electricity
   C sound
   D shaking

18. What form of energy does rubbing hands become?
   A electrical energy
   B stored energy
   C light energy
   D heat energy

19. After a soccer ball is kicked, it eventually stops rolling. Why is this so? The ball
   A stops rolling because of friction.
   B stops after a set amount of time.
   C was not kicked hard enough.
   D is too heavy to keep rolling.

20. Waves in the drawing are moving from left to right. Where will the ball be when the next wave reaches it?

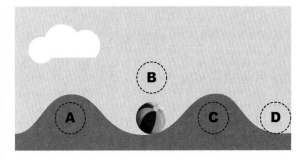

   A
   B
   C
   D

Cooking with the Sun

Did you know that the research NASA uses to launch people into space helps people on Earth? For example, some NASA scientists have the task of developing materials that protect spacecraft and astronauts from heat. Their research produces materials that are lightweight, yet strong and heat-resistant—materials like those needed to protect steelworkers, firefighters, and others.

NASA's scientists can use what they know about heat transfer to help people cook their food. In East Africa, for instance, many people can't find enough wood to cook with.

Square-shaped tiles line the outside of this space shuttle. They resist the heat caused by friction when the spacecraft re-enters the atmosphere.

Using sunlight provides a solution to this problem. Sunlight is a source of energy that can be converted into heat for cooking food. When there is enough sunlight, people can cook with special tools called solar cookers.

NASA has information gathered by satellites about the amount of sunlight that shines in every part of the world. NASA helps people match this information with their exact location. People learn how much solar energy is available for cooking in their area. NASA has helped those in East Africa with a wood shortage problem. Fewer people have to hunt for wood or spend what little money they have on fuel.

With the Sun's energy, East Africans use solar cookers to prepare meals. The Sun is a safe and clean heat source. Solar cooking does not cost much. It does not cause a lot of smoke or air pollution in the environment. Solar cooking helps people harness some of the Sun's energy.

A solar cooker captures sunlight energy to cook food.

Lab zone Take-Home Activity

Would you like to work as a scientist who studies ways to protect workers from too much heat? Or would you rather study new ways to cook food? Tell a partner which job you'd prefer and why.

Electrical Engineer

You know your house needs electricity to run smoothly. Have you ever thought about how important providing electricity is during space missions?

Barbara Kenny has. She is an electrical engineer who works for NASA on ways to change other kinds of energy into electricity to run spacecraft.

While in orbit, for example, a spacecraft spends part of its time in sunlight. Solar panels gather light and change it to electricity used to run the ship. The spacecraft spends the rest of its time in the shadow of the Earth where there is no sunlight. How does it get electricity then?

Dr. Kenny designs generators that make electricity. One kind uses a heavy wheel called a flywheel. While in sunlight, motors make this wheel spin quickly. The energy of motion from spinning is used to generate electricity while the spacecraft is in the dark.

Electrical engineers obtain a degree from a school of engineering.

Dr. Barbara Kenny works with energy forms.

Lab zone Take-Home Activity

If you were an electrical engineer for NASA, what special kind of electrical equipment would you design? How would it be used?

Chapter 2

LIGHT

CALIFORNIA Standards Preview

3PS2.0 Light has a source and travels in a direction. As a basis for understanding this concept:

3PS2.a Students know sunlight can be blocked to create shadows.

3PS2.b Students know light is reflected from mirrors and other surfaces.

3PS2.c Students know the color of light striking an object affects the way the object is seen.

3PS2.d Students know an object is seen when light traveling from the object enters the eye.

3IE5.0 Scientific progress is made by asking meaningful questions and conducting careful investigations. As a basis for understanding this concept and addressing the content in the other three strands, students should develop their own questions and perform investigations. (Also **3IE5.d**, **3IE5.e**)

Standards Focus Questions

• How does light travel?

• What is reflected light?

• What are the colors of objects?

What are some properties of light?

light

opaque

shadow

eye

DIGITAL 9

Chapter 2
Vocabulary

reflect

mirror

absorb   color

Explore How can you make a shadow?

Materials

flashlight

scissors

construction paper

tape

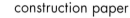

craft stick

What to Do

① Cut out a paper shape. Tape it to a craft stick.

② Shine a flashlight on a wall. Hold your cutout between the light and the wall. **Observe** the shape of the shadow.

③ Move the cutout toward the light. Move it away. How does the shadow's size change? Are its edges sharp or fuzzy?

Be careful!

Use scissors carefully.

Explain Your Results

Predict how can the shadow be changed? Test your prediction. Compare your result with your prediction.

Process Skills

You can use careful **observations** to help you **predict.**

3PS2.0 Light has a source and travels in a direction. **3PS2.a** Students know sunlight can be blocked to create shadows. **3IE5.d** Predict the outcome of a simple investigation and compare the result with the prediction.

How to Read Science

Predict

Predict means to tell what you think might happen next.

Science Article

Carnival Story

Dave needs to hit the wooden penguin with the beanbag. But the penguin might dart behind the cardboard iceberg. If he misses, he won't win a stuffed bear. He takes aim and throws. But the penguin just reaches the iceberg.

Apply It!

Predict what Dave would see or not see when he looks for the penguin after it reaches the iceberg. Make a graphic organizer to help you. Explain your prediction.

I Know → **I Predict**

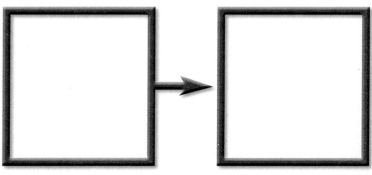

Beams of sunlight shine straight as arrows through the trees. The forest floor is a patchwork of light and shade. In the light, the leaves are green and brilliant. Brightly colored flowers decorate the ground. In the shade, the forest gets less light. Things are hard to see. Plant colors are dull and gray. Why does light make so much difference?

Standards Focus 3PS2.0 Light has a source and travels in a direction. As a basis for understanding this concept:
3PS2.a Students know sunlight can be blocked to create shadows.
3PS2.d Students know an object is seen when light traveling from the object enters the eye.

Lesson 1

How does light travel?

Light is a form of energy. Light travels in a straight line away from its source. When an object blocks light, a shadow forms. You see objects when light travels from the objects and enters your eyes.

The Path of Light

You have learned that the Sun is the main source of energy on Earth. Energy from the Sun comes to Earth as light. **Light** is a form of energy that travels in a straight line away from its source. Light from the Sun moves outward in all directions. Some of this light comes to Earth.

Light from a lamp or a lantern also moves outward in all directions. The light from a flashlight, though, is partly blocked. This is why the light from a flashlight shines in only one direction.

Beams of light travel from their sources in this city.

1. ✓**Checkpoint** How does light travel, starting from its source?

2. ✏️**Writing in Science Narrative** Write a paragraph about observing beams of sunlight.

Light and Shadow

Light strikes objects that are in its path. Some objects stop the light. These objects are called **opaque.** Opaque objects block light. They keep light from passing through. Light cannot bend or turn corners to get around an opaque object. That is because light travels in a straight line.

Shadows form behind objects in the direction away from the light source. A **shadow** is an area that does not receive light directly. Think of an umbrella. A thick umbrella blocks sunlight and rain. It stops either one from traveling any farther in the same direction. You might have used the shadow cast by an umbrella at the beach on a sunny day. Because the area covered in shadow does not get light directly, it is often cooler there.

Kinds of Shadows

Light can cause different kinds of shadows. Light shining directly overhead casts a shadow on the ground that is about the same size as the object that it hits. Light striking from the side of an object casts a shadow on the ground that is a different size.

An umbrella blocks sunlight, forming a shadow.

These shadows are about the same size as the objects because they formed near noon time. How would the shadows look in the late afternoon?

The distance between an object and the surface on which its shadow is seen affects the edges of the shadow. Suppose the surface on which the shadow forms is close to the object. The shadow will have sharp edges. If the surface is far away from the object, the shadow will have fuzzy edges.

The same umbrella blocks rain, forming an area that remains dry.

1. **✓Checkpoint** Why do opaque objects cause shadows?

2. **Predict** A sign is high above the ground. Predict how sharp the edges of its shadow on the ground will be.

TARGET SKILL

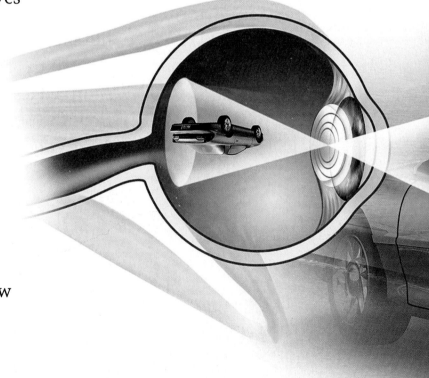

Light from the dog interacts with the eye. The result is an image of the dog on the back of the eye.

What Your Eye Sees

You can see objects because light shines on them. Light traveling from objects enters your eye. The **eye** is the part of your body that is sensitive to light. Light interacts with parts in the eye. Then you see the objects.

Follow the steps that lead to seeing an object. Light first passes through your eye's clear covering. Next, light moves through your eye to the layer in the back of the eye. An upside-down image of the object forms there. The eye then sends a signal to your brain. Finally, the brain flips the image so that you see an image that is right side up. The brain also helps you know what you are seeing.

Light carrying the image of the dog travels from the dog to the eye

Suppose an object, such as a car, gets between you and what you are seeing, such as a dog. Now you can no longer see the dog. This is because the car blocks the light coming from the dog. You can see only the car. This shows how light travels in a straight line.

✓ Lesson Review

1. What must happen in order for you to see an object?

2. Suppose a car comes between you and a dog you were looking at. Why can you no longer see the dog?

3. ✏ **Writing in Science** **Descriptive** Describe what happens when light strikes an opaque object. How does this show that light travels in a straight line?

A car blocks the light coming from the dog. Light from the car interacts with the eye instead.

STATE
ABC-123

What is reflected light?

Light bounces off mirrors and other objects it strikes. The light is reflected. It travels in a straight line in a new direction.

The water of this lake is very smooth. It reflects light coming from the trees like a mirror.

Bouncing Light

Light hitting an object will **reflect**, or bounce off the object. The light that reflects keeps moving in a straight line. The line goes in a different direction than before the light hit the object.

All objects reflect light. This reflected light allows you to see objects. Most of the objects that you see do not make their own light. Light comes from the Sun or other light sources. This light hits objects and then reflects off them. If the reflected light enters your eyes, you see the objects. When you are in a dark room, no light can reflect off objects. This is why you can't see them when the lights are turned off.

Reflection in a Mirror

Some objects have very smooth surfaces. Light coming from an object that reflects from this kind of surface travels together in a new direction. Objects that reflect light in this way are called mirrors. A **mirror** is a surface made of shiny material.

Standards Focus 3PS2.b Students know light is reflected from mirrors and other surfaces.

50

Light from an object that reflects in a mirror might travel to your eye. You can then see the object clearly. The mirror keeps the light from scattering in many directions.

Look at how this light beam travels. The light beam hits the mirror and is reflected back into the room.

The mirror reflects this beam of light in a different direction.

1. **✔ Checkpoint** Compare the light that strikes a flat surface and the light that is reflected from that surface. How are they alike? How are they different?

2. **✏ Writing in Science Personal Letter** Write a letter to a friend about a breeze that changed the calm reflection of things you saw in a pond.

This mirror reflects light from the scissors in one direction to your eyes. You see an image in the mirror.

This rough paper scatters light from the scissors in many directions. You do not see an image in the paper.

Reflection Off Other Surfaces

The surface of an object affects the way that light reflects from it. Many kinds of objects, such as books, do not have smooth surfaces. Light that reflects off such a surface scatters in many different directions. When you look at the object, some of the reflected light enters your eyes. You see only the object. You do not see other objects reflected in it.

Exploring a Reflected Light Beam

The picture on the next page demonstrates reflection and the path of a reflected beam of light. A mist of water was sprayed in a darkened room. The light coming from a flashlight passes straight through the mist. Some of the light strikes the small droplets of water in the air and is reflected. This reflected light moves in all directions. Some of it enters your eyes. You can see an image of the beam. This shows how the light is traveling in a straight line.

A beam of light shines through water mist.

Some of the light strikes water droplets and is reflected back to your eyes.

✓ Lesson Review

1. Why can't you see objects in a completely dark room?

2. Describe how light coming from an object is reflected from a mirror.

3. **Writing in Science Personal Letter** Write a letter to a friend that explains how people see the world around them.

What are the colors of objects?

Sunlight contains all the colors of the rainbow. Objects in sunlight absorb some colors and reflect others. An object's color is the color it reflects. The color of the light that shines on an object affects its color too.

Colors of Objects in Sunlight

Sunlight is made of many different colors of light. They combine to form white light. When sunlight strikes objects, many objects **absorb**, or take in, some of the light. They reflect the rest of the light. The light that reflects from an object determines the **color** of the object. The color is red, yellow, or blue or some combination of these colors. If no light shines on the object, then it has no color!

Sunlight and white light contain all of the colors of the rainbow. Which color in sunlight is reflected from each of these objects?

Standards Focus 3PS2.c Students know the color of light striking an object affects the way the object is seen.

54

Colors Your Eyes See

When light strikes an object, you cannot see the colors the object absorbs. You can only see the color the object reflects. A yellow tulip, for instance, absorbs all colors except yellow. This is the color that is reflected. An object that reflects all colors of sunlight appears white. An object that absorbs all colors appears black.

Exploring Sunlight

The picture shows how colored cellophane can show that different colors of light make up sunlight. A piece of cardboard has sections cut out in the shapes of flower parts. A different colored piece of cellophane is taped behind each flower part section. Held against a window, the flower looks like a stained glass window! Can you list the colors shown? These are some of the colors in sunlight. Each cellophane color allows only that color of light in sunlight to pass through. The other colors are absorbed.

Sunlight shines through the cellophane parts of the flower. Passing sunlight through colored cellophane can create light sources of different colors.

1.  **Checkpoint** Why does white light passing through blue cellophane appear blue?

2. **Writing in Science** **Descriptive** Write about brightly colored objects that you have seen outside. Explain why each object has its color.

Exploring the Effects of Colored Light

You know that the part of sunlight an object reflects determines its color. How will light that is a color other than white affect the object's color? Look at the bird made from white paper. White objects reflect all colors. So if red light shines on the white bird, the bird looks red. The bird reflects the color that shines on it.

Notice how each colored box below has a certain color in white light. How will the boxes appear under different colors of light? The pictures on the next page show some examples.

Blue, green, and red light is each just one part of white light. Each of these colors affects the appearance of the colored boxes.

Light bulbs made of colored glass can show how the color of light affects the way an object is seen.

✔ Lesson Review

1. Why does a white wall appear yellow in the light of a yellow neon sign?

2. Why does a red rose look black or gray under green light?

3. **Predict** Red light and green light combine to form yellow light. Predict what you would see if you shine red light and green light on a white object.

The red, yellow, and blue boxes will appear to have those colors in white light.

Blue light shines on a yellow box. The reflected light appears slightly green.

Green light shines on a red box. The box absorbs most of the light. The box appears gray.

Red light shines on a blue box. The reflected light appears lavender.

Light Reflections

A light beam from a flashlight travels in a straight line. When the light beam strikes a mirror at an angle, it reflects and travels in another direction. If the light beam strikes another mirror at an angle, it reflects again and travels in another direction. In this way a beam of light can travel from mirror to mirror in straight lines.

1 Look at the path made by the reflected light beams. What kind of figure do the beams make together?

A. a 4-sided figure   B. a 5-sided figure

C. a circle   D. a triangle

2 Which of the following could also describe the figure?

A. a sphere   B. a cone

C. a shadow   D. a rectangle

3 Suppose each of the sides of the figure is 64 cm. What is the length of the perimeter?

A. 256 cm   B. 246 cm

C. 128 cm   D. 68 cm

Lab zone Take-Home Activity

Shine a flashlight into a mirror at home. Hold the flashlight so that the beam hits the mirror at different angles. Notice the places where the reflected beam hits the wall. Make drawings to show the paths that the light beam follows.

Investigate How is light reflected by mirrors and other surfaces?

Materials

light viewer
(prepared by teacher)

metric ruler and
white paper

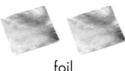

foil

flashlight and mirror

What to Do

1 Hold a flashlight 60 cm from the box. Shine the light through the slits. The black paper stops most of the light, but some light goes through the slits. **Observe** the light's path inside the box.

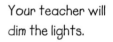

60 cm

Your teacher will dim the lights.

2 Tilt a mirror in the box to reflect the light. Observe the light's path.

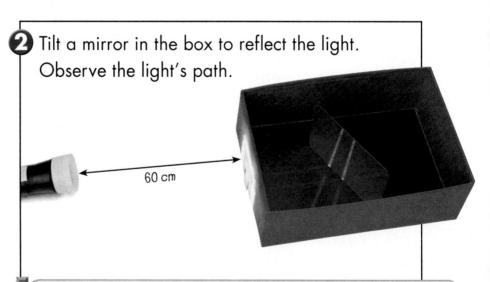

60 cm

Process Skills

You **collect data** when you record what you **observe** in an investigation. When you use your data to **draw a conclusion**, you are **interpreting** your **data.**

3PS2.b Students know light is reflected from mirrors and other surfaces.
3IE5.e Collect data in an investigation and analyze those data to develop a logical conclusion.

3 Draw the path of the light.

4 Find out how light reflects off other surfaces. Try smooth aluminum foil, wrinkled aluminum foil, and white paper.

no object

mirror

smooth foil

wrinkled foil

white paper

Explain Your Results

1. Analyze your **data.** Draw a logical **conclusion.** Describe how light is reflected from the mirror's surface.

2. Compare how light is reflected from a mirror and from other surfaces.

Go Further

What would you see if you sprayed a water mist from a spray bottle over the box?

Focus on the BIG Idea

Light energy travels in a straight line away from its source. Light makes shadows. Sunlight contains many different colors of light. Objects absorb and reflect colors of light.

Lesson 1

How does light travel?

- Light is a form of energy. Light travels from its source in a straight line.
- Some objects block light. Shadows form.
- The direction of light and the position of objects affect shadows.
- Objects are seen when light coming from the objects enters the eye and interacts with it.

Lesson 2

What is reflected light?

- All surfaces reflect light.
- The surface of objects affects the way light is reflected.
- Mirrors have shiny surfaces that reflect light.

Lesson 3

What are the colors of objects?

- Sunlight contains many different colors of light.
- Objects absorb some colors of sunlight. They reflect other colors. The light objects reflect is the color of the objects.
- Colored light affects the appearance of objects.

Cross-Curricular Links

English–Language Arts

Building Vocabulary

Look again at page 40. Identify the picture behind the words *opaque* and *shadow*. Write a paragraph explaining how the terms relate to the picture.

Mathematics

Mirror, Mirror

You count 12 objects reflected in one mirror. How many reflections of the objects would there be if there were 9 mirrors?

Challenge!

Visual and Performing Arts

Mirror Lake

Make a drawing or painting that shows a reflection of the land on the smooth surface of a lake.

Health

Eye Care

Speak with your school nurse or another health care specialist. Find out what you should do to protect your eyes and the care needed to keep your eyes healthy. Write a paragraph describing what you learn.

Use Vocabulary

absorb page 54	**mirror** page 50
color page 54	**opaque** page 46
eye page 48	**reflect** page 50
light page 45	**shadow** page 46

Use the word from the list that completes each sentence. If you can't answer a question, read the listed page again.

1. An object with a shiny surface that reflects light is a(n) _____.

2. Light can _____ off an object.

3. An object has the _____ of the light it reflects.

4. _____ is a form of energy that moves in a straight line.

5. The body part that is sensitive to light energy is the _____.

6. A dark area that does not receive light directly is a(n) _____.

7. An object can _____, or take in, light that strikes it.

8. _____ objects stop light from traveling in the same direction.

Think About It

9. How does light travel away from a source, such as a lamp?

10. Why doesn't sunlight pass through a brick wall?

11. **Process Skills** **Interpret Data** The chart shows colors of a red cup in different colors of light. Explain the noted colors of the cup.

Color of Light	White	Green	Red
Color of Cup	Red	Gray	Red

12. **Predict** A chair in morning sunlight casts a long shadow with a fuzzy edge at the end of it. Predict the kind of shadow it will have at noon. Use the following graphic organizer

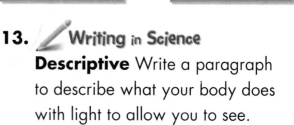

I know → I predict

13. **Writing in Science**

Descriptive Write a paragraph to describe what your body does with light to allow you to see.

California Standards Practice

Write the letter of the correct answer.

14. What does a car blocking a dog from view demonstrate?

    A Light can move around objects.

    B Light turns a different color.

    C Light forms a shadow.

    D Light travels in straight lines.

15. Sunlight shining from above an object forms what kind of shadow?

    A much larger than the object

    B about the same size as the object

    C half the size of the object

    D longer than the object

16. When can you see objects?

    A when objects absorb color

    B when objects absorb light

    C when shadows form

    D when reflected light enters the eye

17. Describe light that reflects off a rough surface.

    A travels in the same direction

    B cannot be absorbed

    C cannot be seen

    D scatters in many directions

18. What will reflect all the colors in sunlight?

    A a blue book

    B a purple flower

    C an orange basketball

    D a white piece of chalk

19. What will absorb all the colors in sunlight?

    A a red rose

    B black pavement

    C a yellow bus

    D a green plant

20. The Sun shines on this table at noon. What will the shadow be like just before sunset?

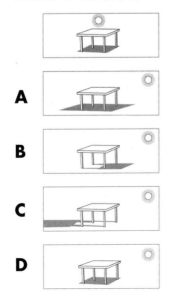

Optometrist

Optometrists help us take care of our eyes. Sometimes people do not see everything clearly. Things that are far away seem blurry to some people. They are nearsighted. Other people have a hard time seeing things up close. They are farsighted. An optometrist can prescribe lenses with the proper shape to correct these problems. The shape of the lens corrects how light enters the eye.

Optometrists can help with other eye problems. They can diagnose and treat some eye diseases. They can check to see how well you see colors. They can also recommend exercises to help your eyes work together better.

If you want to help people see better, you might like to become an optometrist. First, you must earn a college degree. Then you go to optometry school. Finally, you must pass a test given by the state where you want to be an optometrist.

Lab zone Take-Home Activity

The way a camera works is similar to the way an eye works. Find out how a camera and an eye work, and write a paragraph on each.

Chapter 3
Matter

3PS1.0 Energy and matter have multiple forms and can be changed from one form to another. As a basis for understanding this concept:

3PS1.e Students know matter has three forms: solid, liquid, and gas.

3PS1.f Students know evaporation and melting are changes that occur when the objects are heated.

3PS1.g Students know that when two or more substances are combined, a new substance may be formed with properties that are different from those of the original materials.

3PS1.h Students know all matter is made of small particles called atoms, too small to see with the naked eye.

3PS1.i Students know people once thought that earth, wind, fire, and water were the basic elements that made up all matter. Science experiments show that there are more than 100 different types of atoms, which are presented on the periodic table of the elements.

3IE5.0 Scientific progress is made by asking meaningful questions and conducting careful investigations. As a basis for understanding this concept and addressing the content in the other three strands, students should develop their own questions and perform investigations. (Also **3IE5.b**, **3IE5.e**)

Standards Focus Questions

- What makes up matter?
- What are the forms of matter?
- What are chemical changes in matter?

What are objects made of and how do they change?

matter

property

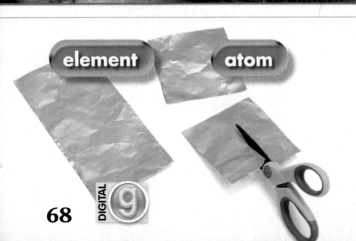

element

atom

periodic table

68

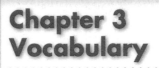

Chapter 3 Vocabulary

evaporation

melting

chemical change

Explore What makes up a magazine picture?

A picture on a magazine cover looks solid and smooth, but not through a 30X microscope.

Materials

picture from a magazine cover

30X microscope

What to Do

1 **Observe** the picture on a magazine cover.

2 Observe with a 30X microscope.

Explain Your Results

Communicate In your opinion did the picture look solid using just your naked eye? What evidence did you **observe** through the 30X microscope? Compare your opinion and your evidence.

3PS1.h Students know all matter is made of small particles called atoms, too small to see with the naked eye. **3IE5.b** Differentiate evidence from opinion and know that scientists do not rely on claims or conclusions unless they are backed by observations that can be confirmed.

How to Read Science

Reading Skills

TARGET SKILL

Sequence

Sequence is the order in which events take place. Clue words such as *first*, *next*, *then*, and *finally* can alert you to the **sequence** of events. They are marked in the brochure below

Brochure

Making Steel

Steel is made from rocks with iron in them. **First,** the rocks are melted with heat to remove waste rock from the iron. **Then** oxygen is bubbled through the melted iron. The melted iron is now steel. **Next,** the steel is poured into molds. **Finally,** the steel cools and hardens into shapes.

This rock has iron in it.

Apply It!

Make a graphic organizer like the one shown. Use it to **communicate** the events when steel is made in the proper order. Write an event after each clue word.

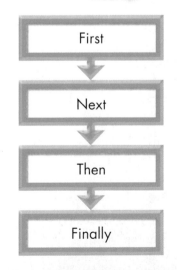

First

Next

Then

Finally

You Are There!

You walk into a room and see all of these objects. Wow! It's a sports lover's dream! You look around for the gear you need for your favorite game. How do you find it among all of this stuff? Well, you look for certain colors, sizes, and shapes. Let's see now . . . Ah! There it is! What makes it different from all the rest?

Standards Focus 3PS1.0 Energy and matter have multiple forms and can be changed from one form to another. As a basis for understanding this concept:

3PS1.h Students know all matter is made of small particles called atoms, too small to see with the naked eye.

3PS1.i Students know people once thought that earth, wind, fire, and water were the basic elements that made up all matter. Science experiments show that there are more than 100 different types of atoms, which are presented on the periodic table of the elements.

DIGITAL

Lesson 1

What makes up matter?

People have thought about matter since ancient times. Matter is made of atoms too small to see with just your eyes. Kinds of matter can be organized by their properties.

A World of Matter

All of the objects you see around you are made of matter. **Matter** is anything that has mass and takes up space. An object's mass is the amount of matter it has. You can feel the mass of objects when you pick them up. When you blow up a balloon, you see that even air is made of matter.

A **property** is something about matter that you can observe with one or more of your senses. A ball, for instance, looks round and may feel either smooth or bumpy. It could be hard or soft. It may feel light or heavy in weight. Whether it bounces or not tells you more about the ball's properties.

These balls, the hockey puck, the baseball mitt, and the air inside the tennis ball are matter.

1. ✓**Checkpoint** What is matter?

2. ✏️**Writing in Science** **Descriptive** Choose an object you see and make a list of its properties. Write a paragraph using the information from your list. Exchange your paragraph with a classmate. Try to guess each other's object.

DIGITAL NSTA SciLinks keyword: matter code: gr3p73

Parts of Matter

Have you used aluminum foil to wrap a sandwich? This foil is made of particles of the element aluminum. An **element** is matter made from a single type of particle that is too small to see.

If you cut a piece of foil in half, both pieces are still made of aluminum. If you cut it in half again, each new piece is also aluminum. No matter how many times you cut the foil, each piece is still made of aluminum.

People in ancient times wondered whether you could keep cutting a substance forever. They thought that an element could be cut into tiny pieces that could not be cut any further. They called these tiny pieces *atoms.*

Matter's Smallest Particles

Today scientists know that all matter is made of atoms. An **atom** is the smallest particle of matter that has the properties of an element. Some matter, such as aluminum, contains only atoms of one element. Other kinds of matter, such as water, are made of atoms of different elements. These atoms act together to give the matter its properties.

A piece of aluminum cut ever smaller is still aluminum.

A microscope is a tool for observing matter up close.

This is a picture of a helmet.

Looking At Parts of Matter

You cannot see single atoms with your eyes. Atoms are so small that scientists form images of them using tools a lot more powerful than the microscope shown on this page. However, the microscope can give the viewer an idea of how atoms combine to form matter. Look what happens when a picture from a magazine is placed under the microscope. The solid colors are actually patterns of tiny dots of only a few colors. These dots combine to make all of the colors in the picture. In the same way, all the different kinds of matter are made of combinations of just a few kinds of atoms.

The microscope has magnified the picture 3 times the original size.

1. ✓**Checkpoint** How are atoms and elements related?

2. 🖊 **Writing in Science Descriptive** Write a report about building a playhouse with wooden blocks of just a few colors. How would matter in a real house be similar?

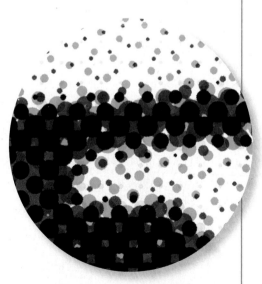

Atoms of matter are like the colored dots that combine to form the picture of the helmet.

Empedocles

Empedocles [em PED uh KLEEZ] lived in ancient Greece. He and others thought that earth, air, fire, and water were the four elements that made up all matter.

Living things are mostly made of carbon, oxygen, nitrogen, and hydrogen atoms.

Changing Ideas About Matter

People in ancient times wondered what matter was made of. They made observations of the world around them. They saw wood burn and turn to ash as gas and smoke rose from a fire. They observed that water evaporated and then fell to Earth as rain. So people once thought that all matter was made out of just four elements: earth, air, fire, and water.

Today, science experiments show that there are more than 100 different elements. Some matter, such as aluminum foil, is made of just one kind of element. But most matter is made of two or more elements.

Scientists arrange the elements in a chart called the **periodic table** of the elements. Elements are arranged in rows and columns according to their properties. The table is shown below. People who discover a new element get to suggest a name for the element. Einsteinium and seaborgium were named for famous scientists. Berkelium and californium were named for the places where they were discovered.

The chart below displays the names and symbols of elements and other information about them.

Periodic Table of the Elements

gold

copper

Form at room temperature
- Gas
- Liquid
- Solid
- Not found in nature

1 H Hydrogen																	2 He Helium
3 Li Lithium	4 Be Beryllium											5 B Boron	6 C Carbon	7 N Nitrogen	8 O Oxygen	9 F Fluorine	10 Ne Neon
11 Na Sodium	12 Mg Magnesium											13 Al Aluminum	14 Si Silicon	15 P Phosphorus	16 S Sulfur	17 Cl Chlorine	18 Ar Argon
19 K Potassium	20 Ca Calcium	21 Sc Scandium	22 Ti Titanium	23 V Vanadium	24 Cr Chromium	25 Mn Manganese	26 Fe Iron	27 Co Cobalt	28 Ni Nickel	29 Cu Copper	30 Zn Zinc	31 Ga Gallium	32 Ge Germanium	33 As Arsenic	34 Se Selenium	35 Br Bromine	36 Kr Krypton
37 Rb Rubidium	38 Sr Strontium	39 Y Yttrium	40 Zr Zirconium	41 Nb Niobium	42 Mo Molybdenum	43 Tc Technetium	44 Ru Ruthenium	45 Rh Rhodium	46 Pd Palladium	47 Ag Silver	48 Cd Cadmium	49 In Indium	50 Sn Tin	51 Sb Antimony	52 Te Tellurium	53 I Iodine	54 Xe Xenon
55 Cs Cesium	56 Ba Barium	71 Lu Lutetium	72 Hf Hafnium	73 Ta Tantalum	74 W Tungsten	75 Re Rhenium	76 Os Osmium	77 Ir Iridium	78 Pt Platinum	79 Au Gold	80 Hg Mercury	81 Tl Thallium	82 Pb Lead	83 Bi Bismuth	84 Po Polonium	85 At Astatine	86 Rn Radon
87 Fr Francium	88 Ra Radium	103 Lr Lawrencium	104 Rf Rutherfordium	105 Db Dubnium	106 Sg Seaborgium	107 Bh Bohrium	108 Hs Hassium	109 Mt Meitnerium	110 Ds Darmstadtium	111 Uuu Unununium	112 Uub Unumbium		114 Uuq Ununquaternium				

57 La Lanthanum	58 Ce Cerium	59 Pr Praseodymium	60 Nd Neodymium	61 Pm Promethium	62 Sm Samarium	63 Eu Europium	64 Gd Gadolinium	65 Tb Terbium	66 Dy Dysprosium	67 Ho Holmium	68 Er Erbium	69 Tm Thulium	70 Yb Ytterbium
89 Ac Actinium	90 Th Thorium	91 Pa Protactinium	92 U Uranium	93 Np Neptunium	94 Pu Plutonium	95 Am Americium	96 Cm Curium	97 Bk Berkelium	98 Cf Californium	99 Es Einsteinium	100 Fm Fermium	101 Md Mendelevium	102 No Nobelium

✓ Lesson Review

1. Explain why most objects you observe are not elements.

2. How are elements arranged in the periodic table?

3. **Sequence** List the steps people in ancient times once used to conclude that matter is made up of small parts. Use a graphic organizer.

TARGET SKILL

Orange juice is a liquid. Its particles can flow past one another.

Lesson 2

What are the forms of matter?

Matter can be in the form of a solid, a liquid, or a gas. Matter can change from one form to another.

Forms of Matter

Most of the matter around you is a solid, a liquid, or a gas. The particles in these three forms of matter are always moving. In some matter particles move very little. In other matter particles move a lot.

Solids

The bowling ball is a solid. It keeps its shape. The particles of a solid are firmly held together. They vibrate, but they stay in place.

Liquids

The orange juice is a liquid. It takes the shape of the glass into which it is poured. When you pour it into another glass, it changes shape. It still takes up the same amount of space. The particles of a liquid are loosely held together. They can flow past one another.

A bowling ball is a solid. Its particles are firmly held together.

Standards Focus **3PS1.e** Students know matter has three forms: solid, liquid, and gas.
3PS1.f Students know evaporation and melting are changes that occur when the objects are heated.

Air being pumped into this ball is a gas. Its tiniest particles are not held together.

Look for Active Art animations at www.pearsonsuccessnet.com

DIGITAL

Gases

The air being pumped into the basketball is a gas. It has no shape of its own. When you pump air into a ball, the air fills the space. Like other gases, air has no shape. The tiny gas particles are not held together. They bounce off one another as they move freely. Unlike solids and liquids, the amount of space that gases take up changes. The particles spread out, or expand, to fill whatever space is available.

1. ✔ **Checkpoint** Identify three forms of matter.

2. ✏ **Writing in Science Descriptive** Describe the differences between matter in brick, water, and air.

Effects of Heat on Liquids

Have you ever used a sponge to clean your kitchen table? As you moved the sponge across the table, water spread over the surface. But a few minutes later, the wet table was dry. What happened to the water? Evaporation happened. The liquid water gained heat energy from its surroundings and turned into a gas. **Evaporation** occurs when a liquid is changed into a gas. When water is in the form of a gas, it is called water vapor. The heat caused the water to change form.

Heat from your body can cause matter to change form too. Has a doctor or nurse ever cleaned your skin with rubbing alcohol? Your body heat makes the alcohol evaporate. As the liquid turns into a gas, it carries away heat. Your skin feels cool.

The gasoline that powers a car also evaporates. This can happen when gasoline flows from the pump into a car. The gasoline vapor has harmful chemicals that can pollute the air. Many gasoline stations have special hoses to catch the vapor. These hoses keep the evaporated gasoline from escaping into the air.

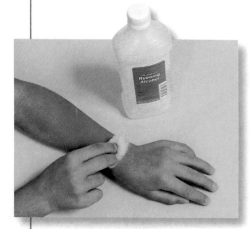

Heat from the body is released as the liquid rubbing alcohol evaporates.

This special hose collects gasoline vapor that can pollute the air.

The liquid water in this flask is evaporating. Water particles separate. Water vapor forms above the liquid water.

Heat causes frozen water, or ice, to melt.

Heat changes dry ice from a solid directly to a gas.

Effects of Heat on Solid Matter

Has an ice cream cone ever turned to liquid in your hand on a hot day? If so, you know that heat energy can change solids into liquids. For instance, ice is water in solid form. When the temperature of the air is above 0°C (32°F), ice melts. **Melting** is changing from a solid to a liquid. Under normal conditions, most solids have a certain temperature at which they melt.

Removing heat can cause even gases to become solids. Carbon dioxide, for instance, is a gas at room temperature. If the gas loses enough heat energy, it becomes the solid called dry ice. If dry ice gains heat energy, it can become a gas without first becoming a liquid.

1. ✓**Checkpoint** Compare water that evaporates with ice that melts.

TARGET SKILL

2. **Sequence** Use a graphic organizer to list the steps you would use to evaporate a small amount of water.

Effects of Heat on Metals

Water is not the only thing that changes form when heat energy is added or taken away. Other materials, such as rock and metal, can also change form. It is much hotter deep inside Earth than it is at the surface. In fact, part of Earth's core is melted iron metal. Heat inside Earth can cause rock to melt too. The hot liquid rock that forms is called *magma*. Magma can move upward through cracks in the Earth and erupt from volcanoes.

Magma that erupts from a volcano is called *lava*. On Earth's surface, the liquid lava loses heat energy. It changes form and becomes solid rock. Sometimes this rock builds up into volcanic mountains.

This river of hot liquid rock lost heat energy and changed from a liquid to solid rock.

Heat was used to make this metal beam. Beams like this are found in many buildings. Many items in your home are made from metal that was once melted. Examples include pots, pans, and even paper clips.

People have learned how to use heat to change matter. For example, two pieces of metal can be joined through welding. Welding heats the pieces of metal until they melt. When they cool, they are joined together. The heat can cause some metal to turn to a gas that is dangerous to breathe.

Most metals occur naturally as part of rock. Heat is used to prepare the metal. Rocks with iron, for instance, are mixed with solid fuel and heated in a furnace until the rocks melt. The heat removes some of the rock in the form of a gas. Other waste is poured off. Blowing oxygen through the melted iron turns it into steel. The melted steel is finally allowed to cool and harden.

Each kind of metal melts at a certain temperature.

✓ Lesson Review

1. What causes matter to be in a solid, liquid, or gas state?

2. Why do ice cubes melt when left in a warm room?

3. ✎ **Writing in Science Descriptive** Use the library-media center to learn more about how steel is made. Write a report describing what you would see if you visited a steel plant.

Lesson 3

What are chemical changes in matter?

Some changes in matter can produce new kinds of matter. We use these changes all the time.

Forming Different Materials

Mmmmm. . . There's nothing like the smell of fresh, warm bread. It tastes so good right out of the oven. But you wouldn't want to eat it before it was baked. A bowl of flour, yeast, baking powder, and eggs wouldn't taste very good.

In a **chemical change,** one kind of matter changes into a different kind of matter. A chemical change happens when bread is baked. The batter is a mixture of ingredients. The heat of the oven causes chemical changes to happen. Then a new substance, bread, forms.

A chemical change happens when eggs are cooked. Cooked eggs cannot return to the form of raw eggs.

Baking bread causes a chemical change. A new kind of matter is formed. You cannot get the ingredients back.

Standards Focus 3PS1.g Students know that when two or more substances are combined, a new substance may be formed with properties that are different from those of the original materials.

Remember that after liquid water freezes into ice, the ice can melt back to water. This is because liquid water and solid ice are different forms of the same matter. What about bread? Can bread change back into flour, yeast, baking powder, and eggs? It probably can't. Materials that have gone through a chemical change usually cannot be changed back to the original kind of matter.

Think of a rusty chain, like the one in the picture. Chain links are made of iron. Aided by water, oxygen gas combines with the iron. A chemical change occurs that turns the iron to rust. The rust is a different kind of matter. It cannot easily change back to iron.

A campfire is another example of chemical change. You start with a pile of sticks. Oxygen in the air combines with the wood as it burns. The wood and oxygen change into ashes and other kinds of gas. These are new kinds of matter. The ashes will not turn back into sticks.

Some of the iron in this chain has turned to rust. Rust and iron have different properties.

Burning a wax candle forms black soot on this glass lamp. Wax and soot have different properties.

1. **✓ Checkpoint** What happens during a chemical change?

2. **✎ Writing in Science Personal Letter** Write a letter to a friend explaining what causes a bicycle to rust.

Mixing Matter

Have you ever made a salad? If so, you probably washed the ingredients and cut them into smaller pieces. Then you combined all of the ingredients and mixed them together. Each ingredient in the finished salad kept its original properties. The ingredients did not combine to form new kinds of matter. The lettuce still looked and tasted like lettuce. The carrots still looked and tasted like carrots.

Something quite different happens when you combine vinegar and baking soda. A change produces froth and bubbles that you can see. These are new kinds of matter. Their properties are different from those of vinegar and baking soda.

Two Kinds of Changes

The two examples above show the difference between a physical change and a chemical change. Cutting up food to make a salad changes the shape of the food. That is a physical change. The parts of the salad do not react with one another. They remain the same type of matter.

Adding vinegar to baking soda, however, changes the original materials. New matter forms with different properties. For example, the gas carbon dioxide is made. Carbon dioxide pushes the cork out of the bottle in the picture. The gas then escapes into the air.

The ingredients in trail mix do not change into new kinds of matter.

When vinegar and baking soda are combined, a chemical change happens. New kinds of matter with different properties form.

1. ✔**Checkpoint** What are three examples of chemical changes? How do you know that they are chemical changes?

2. **Sequence** List the steps that describe what happens when vinegar and baking soda are combined. Use a graphic organizer.

You can still tell what ingredients were used to make this salad. After being mixed together, the ingredients keep their original properties.

Using Chemical Changes

You use chemical changes every day. From cooking and eating pizza to watching a fireworks show, chemical changes are part of daily life.

Chemical changes start in your mouth the moment you begin to chew a piece of food. Then more changes happen as the food goes through your body. Chemical changes give your body the material it needs for energy and growth.

Chemical changes help move you from place to place. When gasoline burns, a chemical change releases energy that runs the car's engine.

Chemical changes help us get things clean. For example, chemicals that break down stains are often added to soaps. These stain removers use chemical changes to make clothes and dishes look like new.

Chemical changes in batteries produce electricity in flashlights.

Chemicals added to soaps break down grease and stains.

Burning gasoline in cars causes a chemical change.

Chemical changes can help make sounds that you enjoy. When you flick the switch on a CD player, for example, chemicals combine inside batteries. New substances form. The chemical change makes a small amount of electricity to help you hear your favorite music.

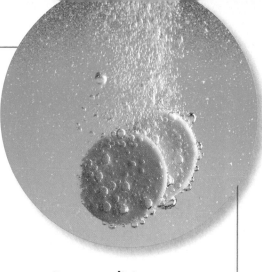

Some medicine tablets for an upset stomach combine with water. Bubbles of gas form.

Chemical changes turn milk into cheese, like these large wheels of cheese at a factory.

✓ **Lesson Review**

1. What are four ways that chemical changes are useful?

2. Does using a battery cause a physical change or a chemical change? Explain your answer.

3. **Writing in Science Descriptive** Describe something you did this week that was made possible or easier by a chemical change.

Measuring Matter

Different tools and different units are used to measure volume, length, and mass.

1 CUP — 250ml
3/4 — 200
— 150
1/2 CUP — 100
1/4 — 50

ml
100
90
80
70
60
50
40
30
20
10

Volume is the amount of space that matter takes up. The volume of the liquid in the measuring cup is 90 milliliters. The graduated cylinder contains the same amount of liquid.

Length is the distance between the two ends of an object. You can use a ruler to measure length. The small marks on the ruler mark off millimeters. There are 10 millimeters in 1 centimeter, so you can count by tens to find the length in millimeters. The paper clip is 30 millimeters long.

Eraser

The paper clip is 3 centimeters long.

CM 0 1 2 3 4 5 6 7 8 9 10 11 12 13 14 15 16 17

30 29 28 27 26 25 24 23 22 21 20 19 18 17 16 15 14 13

DIGITAL

Mass is the amount of matter an object has. You can use a balance to measure mass. The number of plastic 1-gram blocks it takes to balance the pans equals the mass of the object. The eraser is 10 grams.

Use the pictures to answer the questions.

1 The eraser is more than 6 centimeters but less than 7 centimeters long. What is its length in millimeters?

A. 6 mm

B. 65 mm

C. 650 mm

D. 6000 mm

2 5 erasers that are 10 grams each would have what total mass?

A. 500 Kg

B. 5000 g

C. 50 g

D. 5 Kg

3 Which item has the greatest volume?

A. 1 L of milk

B. 500 mL of milk

C. 50 mL of milk

D. 5 mL of milk

Lab zone Take-Home Activity

Use a metric ruler to measure the length of objects in your home. Compare your measurements and order them from shortest to longest.

91

Investigate How can matter change?

Materials

safety goggles

small measuring cup

plastic cup and spoon

glue

food coloring (optional)

borax solution

Process Skills

During an **investigation,** you make **observations** and **collect data.** You can analyze your data to help draw a conclusion.

What to Do

1 Put 30 mL of glue into a cup. You can add food coloring.

2 Add 15 mL of borax solution. Stir.

3PS1.g Students know that when two or more substances are combined, a new substance may be formed with properties that are different from those of the original materials. **3IE5.e** Collect data in an investigation and analyze those data to develop a logical conclusion.

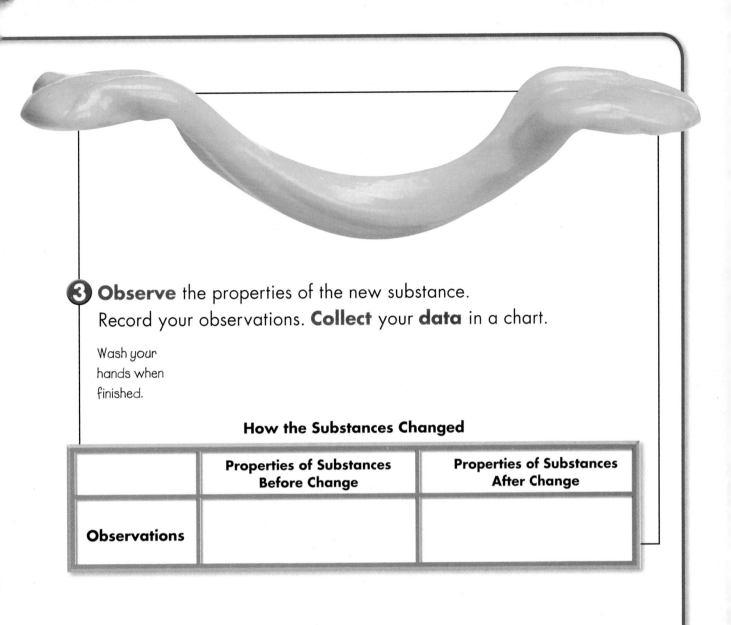

3 **Observe** the properties of the new substance. Record your observations. **Collect** your **data** in a chart.

Wash your hands when finished.

How the Substances Changed

	Properties of Substances Before Change	Properties of Substances After Change
Observations		

Explain Your Results

1. **Analyze** your **data.** Tell if a newly formed substance can have different properties from those of the original materials. Tell how your data supports your conclusion.

2. **Classify** the changes. Was it a physical change or a chemical change?

Go Further

Suppose you used a different amount of borax solution. Would the property of the new substance be different? Design a safe investigation to find out.

Focus on the BIG Idea

Objects are made of atoms of matter. The forms of matter are solid, liquid, and gas, which can change when objects are heated. Matter can combine, forming substances with different properties.

Lesson 1

What makes up matter?

- Matter is anything that takes up space and has mass.
- All matter is made of small particles called atoms. They are too small to see with the eyes alone.
- The Periodic Table of the Elements gives information about the more than 100 different kinds of known elements.

Lesson 2

What are the forms of matter?

- The forms of matter are solid, liquid, and gas.
- A solid has a definite shape. Particles of a solid vibrate in place.
- A liquid does not have a definite shape. Particles of a liquid can flow past one another.
- A gas has no definite shape. Particles of a gas bounce off one another and move freely.
- To change form, matter must gain or lose heat energy.
- Evaporation and melting are changes that occur when objects are heated.

Lesson 3

What are chemical changes in matter?

- In a chemical change, one kind of matter changes into a different kind of matter with new properties.
- Materials that go through a chemical change often cannot be changed back to the original kind of matter.

Cross-Curricular Links

English–Language Arts

Building Vocabulary

Look again at page 69. Identify the pictures behind the words *melting* and *evaporation*. Write a paragraph explaining what these words mean and how they are related.

Mathematics

Heat and Matter

Charcoal melts at 3,500°C. Aluminum foil melts at 660°C. An iron nail melts at 1,535°C. Arrange these kinds of matter from the highest to lowest melting points. Which has the highest melting point? Find the difference between the highest melting point and the lowest melting point.

Challenge!

Visual and Performing Arts

Matter on Stage

Work with a small group of your classmates. Have some students show how particles move in a solid. Have others show how particles move in liquids and gases.

English–Language Arts

Iron Story

Iron is an element used to make many different products. Use the library-media center to learn more about the uses of iron. Then write a story describing how your life would be different if you could not use these iron-containing products.

Chapter 3 Review/Test

Use Vocabulary

atom page 74	**matter** page 73
chemical change page 84	**melting** page 81
element page 74	**periodic table** page 77
evaporation page 80	**property** page 73

Fill in the blanks with the correct vocabulary terms. If you have trouble answering a question, read the listed page again.

1. Anything that has mass and takes up space is _____.

2. A(n) _____ causes one kind of matter to change into another kind.

3. A(n) _____ is the smallest particle of matter with properties of an element.

4. Something about matter that you can observe with one or more of your senses is a(n) _____.

5. _____ occurs when a liquid changes into a gas.

6. A(n) _____ is matter made of one kind of particle too small to see.

7. _____ is a solid changing to a liquid.

Think About It

8. Why are there more kinds of matter than kinds of elements?

9. Why do solids have a definite shape and gases do not?

10. **Process Skills** **Form Questions** What are three questions you could answer by reading the periodic table?

11. **Classify** Classify the following as solids, liquids, or gases: ice, gasoline, oxygen, wood, magma, water vapor.

12. **Sequence** Make a graphic organizer like the one shown. Use it to show steps forming solid water from liquid water.

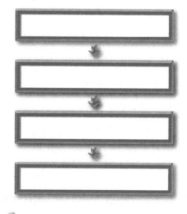

13. **Writing in Science**
Descriptive Describe how our understanding of matter has changed from ancient times to the present.

California Standards Practice

Write the letter of the correct answer.

14. What is the smallest particle of aluminum that still has the properties of aluminum?

   A vinegar

   B an atom

   C rust

   D magma

15. According to people in ancient times, what were the basic elements of matter?

   A the elements of the periodic table

   B gold and silver

   C solids, liquids, and gases

   D earth, air, fire, and water

16. Which of the following is a chemical change?

   A water freezing

   B paper tearing

   C ice melting

   D iron rusting

17. What happens when matter melts?

   A A solid becomes a liquid.

   B A liquid becomes a gas.

   C A gas becomes a liquid.

   D A liquid becomes a solid.

18. About how many different elements are there?

   A 3

   B 5

   C 100

   D 500

19. What happens in a chemical change?

   A The amount of matter changes.

   B The kind of matter changes.

   C Matter freezes.

   D Matter melts.

20. What may have happened to the rubbing alcohol after a few days?

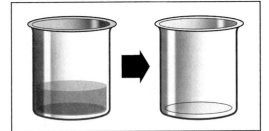

   A It froze.

   B It evaporated.

   C It underwent a chemical change.

   D It melted.

Chemist

Do you like to cook? When you cook you use chemistry. Chemistry is the study of substances and how they change. You might not want to eat all the ingredients separately. After they are mixed and baked, however, they change. Then they taste just right.

Chemists also study the properties of substances. Materials differ, for instance, in their ability to mix together. Honey dissolves in water. Vegetable oil does not. These properties interest Dr. John Pojman. He is a chemistry professor at the University of Southern Mississippi doing research for NASA. Dr. Pojman directs experiments that are done in space where gravity won't interfere. He and other scientists are developing experiments to find out more about the ways that liquids mix together.

Chemists earn a degree in chemistry. Then they work for companies that make food, plastics, medicines, and other products.

Dr. John Pojman directs experiments with fluids in low-gravity conditions.

Lab zone Take-Home Activity

Get permission to mix some cooking oil and water. How well do they mix together? What does the mixture look like? Predict how well they would mix together in space.

Unit A Summary

Chapter 1

How does energy move and change form?
- Energy is the ability to do work. Energy causes changes in objects.
- Energy can be stored and released as heat, light, and motion.
- Energy has many forms and can be changed from one form to another.
- Energy can be carried from one place to another.

Chapter 2

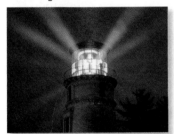

What are some properties of light?
- Light is a form of energy that has a source and travels in a direction.
- Objects reflect and absorb light. Objects are seen when light traveling from objects enters the eye.
- Light of different colors can change the appearance of objects.

Chapter 3

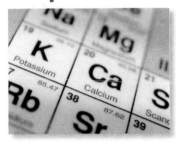

What are objects made of and how do they change?
- Matter has mass and takes up space. Matter has properties that can be observed. Matter is made of particles too small to see with the unaided eye.
- Matter can be in the form of a solid, liquid, or gas. Matter can change form when it is heated or cooled.
- Matter can change to form new kinds of matter with different properties.

Experiment How does energy affect the distance a toy car travels?

When you pull back a pullback car, you wind up its spring. You give the car stored energy. The wound-up spring stores the energy. When you let the car go, the energy stored in the spring turns the gears and makes the car move. Energy stored in the spring changes into energy of motion as the car begins to move.

Materials

meterstick

pullback toy car

masking tape

Process Skills

Scientific progress is made by asking questions and conducting **experiments.** In every experiment you make a **hypothesis,** a testable statement.

Ask a question.

How does a car's stored energy affect the distance it can travel?

State a hypothesis.

If a pullback car's stored energy is increased, then will the distance it can move increase, decrease, or remain about the same? Write your **hypothesis.**

Identify and control variables.

You will change the amount of stored energy your toy car has before it begins to move. You do this by changing the distance you pull the car back. You will measure the distance the car travels. Everything else must stay the same.

3PS1.c Students know machines and living things convert stored energy to motion and heat. **3IE5.0** Scientific progress is made by asking meaningful questions and conducting careful investigations. As a basis for understanding this concept and addressing the content in the other three strands, students should develop their own questions and perform investigations. **3IE5.a** Repeat observations to improve accuracy and know that the results of similar scientific investigations seldom turn out exactly the same because of differences in the things being investigated, methods being used, or uncertainty in the observation. **3IE5.b** Differenciate evidence from opinions and know that scientists do not rely on claims or conclusions unless they are backed by observations that can be confirmed. **3IE5.c** Use numerical data in describing and comparing objects, events, and measurements.

Test your hypothesis.

1 Make a starting line with masking tape.

2 Put down another piece of tape and mark it at 0, 5, 10, 15, 20, 25, and 30 cm.

3 Put the front of the car at the 5 cm line.

4 Pull the car back until the front of the car is at the starting line and let it go.

5 **Measure** the distance the car travels. Record the distance.

6 Repeat steps 3 to 5 but use the 10, 15, 20, 25, and 30 cm lines. Record your data each time.

What happens to the car's stored energy when you let it go?

How does the speed of the car change?

What causes the car to stop?

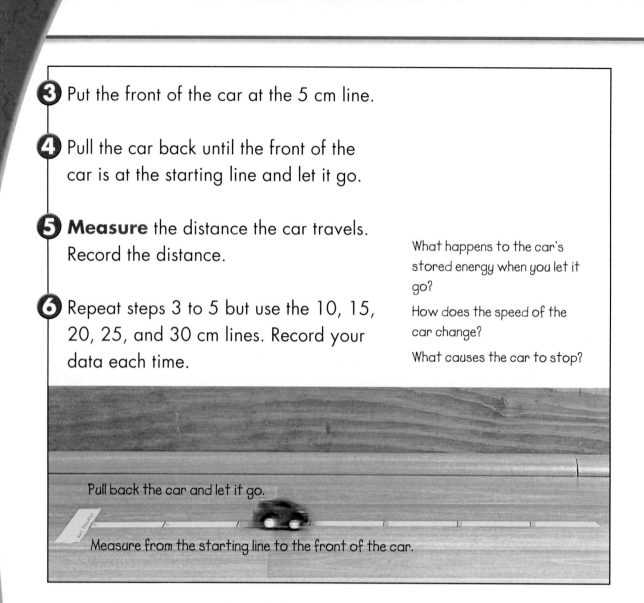

Pull back the car and let it go.

Measure from the starting line to the front of the car.

Collect and record your data.

Distance Moved by Pullback Car	
Distance Pulled Back (cm)	**Distance Traveled** (cm)
0	0
5	
10	
15	
20	
25	
30	

Find a pattern in your chart or graph.
Make a **prediction**.
How far would your car go if you pulled it back 35 cm? Test your prediction.

Interpret your data.

Use your data to make a bar graph. Look at your graph closely. Did the number of centimeters you pulled the car back affect the distance it traveled? Explain. How do your **observations** provide the evidence for your explanation?

How does evidence differ from opinion?

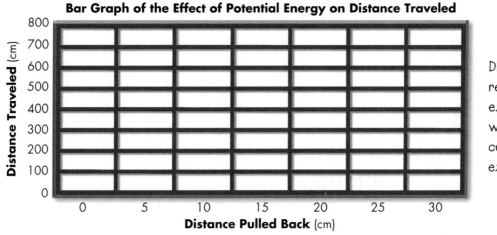

Bar Graph of the Effect of Potential Energy on Distance Traveled

Distance Traveled (cm) — 0, 100, 200, 300, 400, 500, 600, 700, 800

Distance Pulled Back (cm) — 0, 5, 10, 15, 20, 25, 30

Discuss your results and explanations with others and consider their explanations.

Why might different groups get different results? Try the activity again. Repeating the activity may help improve the accuracy of your results.

State your conclusion.

How does increasing a toy car's stored energy affect the distance it can travel? Compare your hypothesis with your results. **Communicate** your conclusion.

---Go Further---

Suppose you add more mass to the car. How would this affect the distances it travels? Make and carry out a plan to answer this or another question you may have.

Show What You Know

Use Light Energy

Use a shallow pan filled with water and a piece of clear plastic wrap to show how the energy from sunlight can change matter. Set the pan in a place that receives direct sunlight. Cover the pan with the plastic wrap. Write a prediction of how the energy of sunlight will affect the liquid water.

After an hour, observe the covered pan. Write a description of what you see.

- Do your observations support your prediction?
- What would happen if you removed the plastic wrap from the pan?

Toy Power

Choose a toy that shows energy changing form. Look for ways the toy also transfers energy from one part to another. Observe the toy as it works. Make a poster that describes the changes from one form of energy to another that you see.

- Where in the toy might there be energy that is stored?
- Where in the toy might there be electric current, light, or energy of motion?
- How might some energy of motion be transferred from one part to another?

Write Narrative Nonfiction

Choose one topic you have learned about in this unit. Examples include elements, light, forms of energy, or ways energy is carried from one place to another. Write and illustrate a picture book for younger children explaining the topic. Remember that narrative nonfiction tells a true story.

Read More About Physical Sciences

Look at other books about physical sciences in your library.
One book you may want to read is:

Changing from solids to liquids to gases
by Dr. Brian Knapp

This book explores how heat affects objects.
Many drawings, and photographs illustrate
ways solids turn to liquids and then to gases.
Matter can also turn from gases to liquids
and then to solids.

Science Fair Projects

Full Inquiry

What effect does the Sun's energy have?

Sunlight changes to other forms of energy, such as heat and motion.

Idea: Use plastic jars to test the effect of energy in sunlight. Use sealable, clear plastic jars, white construction paper, and thermometers. Write a hypothesis that explains what happens when light is let into a jar. Be sure to record and analyze enough data.

How can you change shadows?

Shadows can have different lengths.

Idea: Write a hypothesis explaining how changing the position of light can change the length of a shadow. Make a plan to test your hypothesis.

How does heat affect evaporation?

Liquids evaporate when heated.

Idea: Place identical amounts of water in places that differ in temperature. Make a plan to compare how long it takes for the water to evaporate in each place.

Using Scientific Methods
1. Ask a question.
2. State a hypothesis.
3. Identify and control variables.
4. Test your hypothesis.
5. Collect and record your data.
6. Interpret your data.
7. State your conclusion.
8. Go further.

Unit A California Standards Practice

Write the letter of the correct answer.

1. **When sunlight strikes Earth, most of it changes to which form of energy?**
   - **A** light
   - **B** motion
   - **C** electrical
   - **D** heat

2. **What kind of energy is in a battery?**
   - **A** stored energy
   - **B** light energy
   - **C** heat energy
   - **D** motion energy

3. **Which tool helps change stored food energy to energy of motion?**

   A
   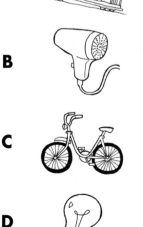

   B

   C

   D

4. **Which of the following transfers energy of motion?**
   - **A** turning on a television
   - **B** lighting a candle
   - **C** burning wood
   - **D** kicking a soccer ball

5. **Friction can change energy of motion into which form of energy?**
   - **A** chemical energy
   - **B** stored fuel energy
   - **C** heat energy
   - **D** stored food energy

Unit A California Standards Practice

6. **Which of the following carries energy from one place to another place?**
   A food
   B gasoline
   C batteries
   D water waves

7. **How does light energy travel?**
   A through opaque objects
   B in circles
   C in straight lines
   D around objects

8. **Which of the following is an opaque object?**
   A glass window
   B clear plastic bag
   C magnifier
   D paperback book

9. **On which part of the eye does an upside-down image form?**

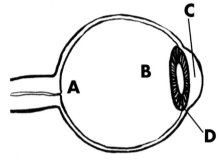

   A A
   B B
   C C
   D D

10. **What happens to a light beam that strikes a mirror?**
   A It is absorbed.
   B It changes color.
   C It is reflected in a straight line in a new direction.
   D All of it changes to heat.

Unit A California Standards Practice

11. What affects the color of an object?

   A the color of the light

   B The object's shadow

   C the object's shape

   D the object's size

12. Which of the following absorbs all colors of light except yellow?

   A an apple

   B a cherry

   C a plum

   D a banana

13. All matter is made of which of the following?

   A properties

   B atoms

   C metal

   D solids

14. Which change shows why people long ago thought that matter was made of earth, air, fire, and water?

   A mixing a salad

   B burning a log

   C cutting an apple

   D making trail mix

15. What describes particles in solids?

   A held so firmly that they cannot vibrate

   B able to move about freely

   C able to flow past one another

   D vibrate in place

Unit A California Standards Practice

16. What causes the water in the drawing to change from A to B?

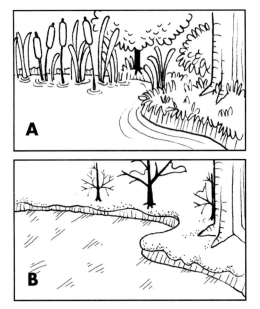

A The water loses heat energy.

B The water gains atoms.

C The water evaporates.

D The water becomes a new kind of matter.

17. What happens when a liquid evaporates?

A It changes into a liquid.

B It changes into a gas.

C It remains a liquid.

D It changes into a solid.

18. Which of the following is a chemical change?

A a salad being mixed

B water evaporating

C wood burning

D water freezing

19. What happens to matter that goes through a physical change?

A It changes into a new kind of matter.

B It gains or loses mass.

C It no longer takes up space.

D It remains the same kind of matter.

20. What must occur for energy to be released inside a battery?

A a chemical change

B evaporation

C loss of heat energy

D a physical change

CALIFORNIA

CALIFORNIA
Unit B

Life Sciences

Joshua Tree

NATIONAL PARK

Southern California

Would you like to observe two different desert environments? If so, plan a visit to Joshua Tree National Park. The park is located near Palm Springs, California. The eastern half of the park is part of the Colorado Desert. Spiky ocotillo plants and cholla cactus grow in this dry environment. The western half of the park is in the Mojave Desert. Here you will find forests filled with the park's namesake—the Joshua tree. Many people think the branches of these trees look like arms pointing to the sky. Early settlers to the area made fences and corrals from the tree's trunk and branches. Native Americans used the tree's strong leaves to make baskets and sandals. Today the Joshua tree provides food and shelter for many kinds of birds, mammals, and insects.

Find Out More

Find out more about deserts in California.

- How have people changed the Colorado and Mojave Deserts? Make a poster or presentation summarizing the changes.

- How do plants and animals survive in the desert? Choose a plant or animal. Find out where it lives and how it survives. Write a report about the plant or animal.

- Visit a desert area or a museum with displays about deserts. Before you go, write five questions you want to answer. Look for the answers during your visit.

Joshua Tree National Park

Chapter 4
Living in Different Environments

CALIFORNIA Standards Preview

3LS1.0 Adaptations in physical structure or behavior may improve an organism's chance for survival. As a basis for understanding this concept:

3LS3.a. Students know plants and animals have structures that serve different functions in growth, survival, and reproduction.

3LS3.b. Students know examples of diverse life forms in different environments, such as oceans, deserts, tundra, forests, grasslands, and wetlands.

3IE5.0 Scientific progress is made by asking meaningful questions and conducting careful investigations. As a basis for understanding this concept and addressing the content in the other three strands, students should develop their own questions and perform investigations. (Also, **3IE5.a**, **3IE5.c**, **3IE5.e**)

Standards Focus Questions

- What structures help plants and animals live and grow?
- What are different environments where things live?
- How do living things survive in places with few trees?
- How do living things survive in forests?
- How do living things survive in water environments?

113

What are ways living things survive in their environments?

adaptation

grassland

desert

DIGITAL
9

Chapter 4 Vocabulary

biome

tundra

wetland

Explore Which bird bill can crush seeds?

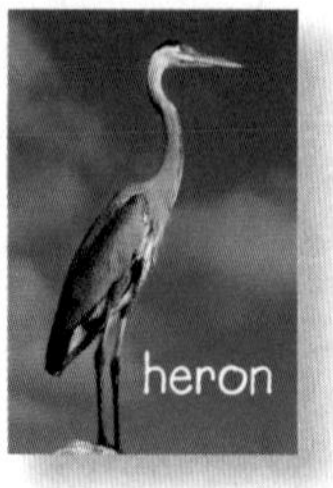

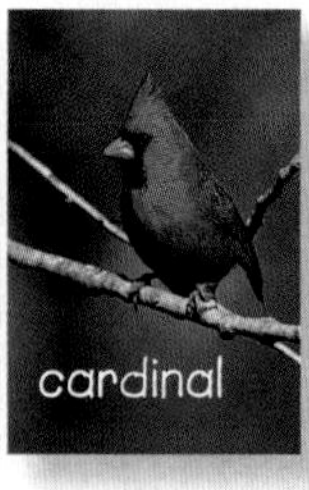

The structure of a bird's bill helps it get the food it needs to survive.

heron   cardinal

Materials

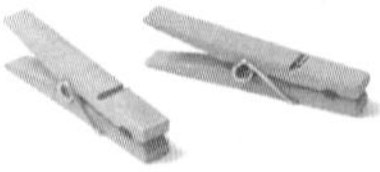

2 clothespins

4 pieces of straw

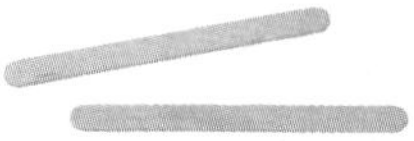

2 craft sticks

glue

What to Do

1 Make the model of a heron's bill shown below. Glue 2 craft sticks to a clothespin. Use the other clothespin as a model of a cardinal's bill. Use a piece of straw as a model of a seed.

2 Use the heron's bill. Pick up a seed. Does the bill crush the seed? Try 5 times. **Collect and record** your **data.** Repeat with the cardinal's bill.

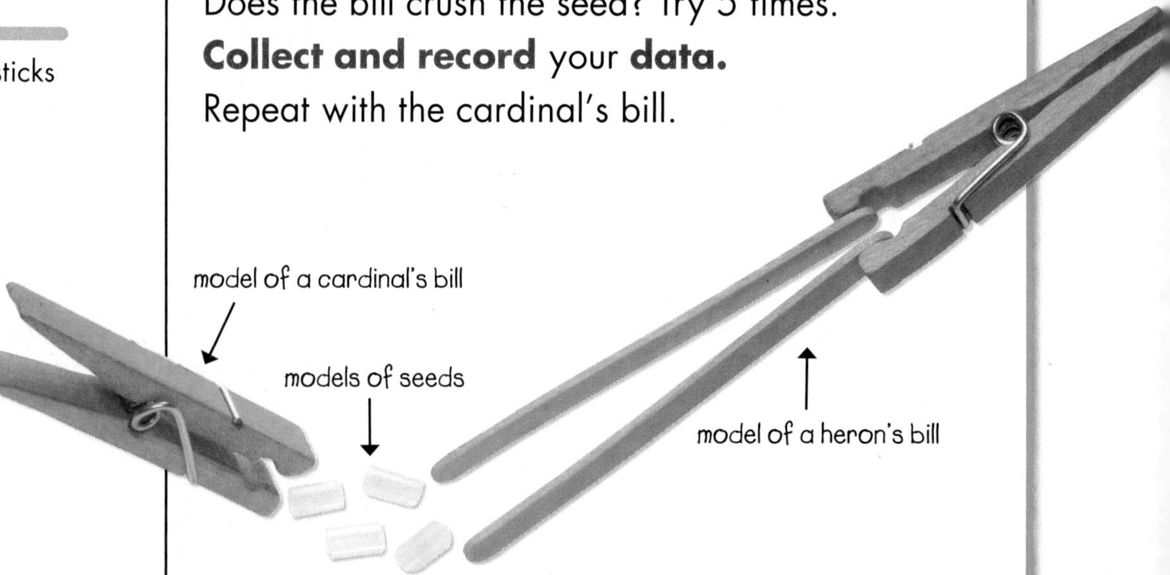

model of a cardinal's bill

models of seeds

model of a heron's bill

Explain Your Results

Draw a Conclusion Which bird crushes seeds? How might crushing seeds help the bird survive?

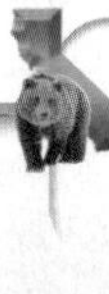

3LS3.0 Adaptations in physical structure or behavior may improve an organism's chance for survival. **3LS3.a** Students know plants and animals have structures that serve different functions in growth, survival, and reproduction. **3IE5.e** Collect data in an investigation and analyze those data to develop a logical conclusion. (Also **3IE5.a**)

How to Read Science

Main Idea and Details

A number of different facts might support a main idea. These facts are called details. Learning to find the **main idea and details** helps you understand what you read. Details in what you read are like **data** you collect in an investigation. The main idea is like a **conclusion** you develop from the data. Study the main idea and details in the graphic organizer below.

Main Idea

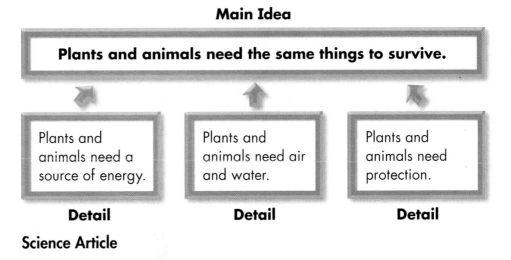

Plants and animals need the same things to survive.

| Plants and animals need a source of energy. | Plants and animals need air and water. | Plants and animals need protection. |
| **Detail** | **Detail** | **Detail** |

Science Article

Home Address

Each kind of animal has a different body covering. A deer in the woods has fur for warmth. A fish in a lake has slippery scales for moving fast through the water. Each kind of covering helps the animal to live where it does.

Apply It!

Make a graphic organizer like the one above. Use it to organize the main idea and details from the science article.

You Are There!

It's early morning in the forest. A row of ants is marching past your feet. You stand very still, listening and watching. Suddenly, you see what looks like two dogs walking through a grassy field. As you look again, you realize that they are not dogs. You've spotted a wolf and her pup! You hear the grass rustle as they scurry out of sight. Animals and plants come in many shapes and sizes, but do they need the same basic things to live?

Standard Focus 3LS1.0 Adaptations in physical structure or behavior may improve an organism's chance for survival. As a basis for understanding this concept:
3LS3.a Students know plants and animals have structures that serve different functions in growth, survival, and reproduction.

DIGITAL

What structures help plants and animals live and grow?

Plants and animals have structures and abilities that help them to survive.

What Living Things Need

Living things need food, air, water, and space to live and grow. Most living things need to protect themselves from things that eat them. They also need to produce offspring.

Plants use energy from the Sun and carbon dioxide from the air to make their own food. Most plants also need water and nutrients from the soil.

Animals cannot make food, so they must eat plants or other animals to get energy and nutrients. Animals get water from drinking or from food. All animals need oxygen from the air or from water. Animals also need to build or find shelter. Shelters protect animals from the weather and other animals.

Animals have structures that help them to meet their needs. Examples of structures include legs, wings, or fins with which to move.

1. **✓Checkpoint** How are the needs of plants and animals alike and different?

2. **Writing in Science Formal Letters** Write a letter to a pet owner explaining what a dog or a cat needs to grow.

Adaptations

Plants and animals live in many different kinds of places. Each kind of plant or animal has features and abilities fitted for where it lives. A structure or ability that helps a living thing meet its needs is an **adaptation.** An adaptation helps a living thing grow, survive, and reproduce.

Adaptations For Getting Food

Animals have different adaptations for getting food. Birds that live in water often have webbed feet for swimming. Hawks and eagles have talons on their feet that grasp food tightly after they swoop down and catch it. Porcupines and hyenas have teeth to handle the kinds of foods they eat.

This porcupine skull shows adaptations of a plant-eating animal. Sharp front teeth cut off parts of plants. Flat teeth in the back of the jaw move from side to side, grinding tough plant material.

This hyena skull shows adaptations of a meat-eating animal. Sharp front teeth tear off meat, and back teeth shred it.

A pouch hangs from the bill of a pelican. When a pelican swoops into the water for food, the pouch acts like a net to help the bird catch fish.

A long, curved bill helps the flamingo filter food from shallow water.

A short, strong bill helps the cardinal break open seeds.

Bird Bill Adaptations

Birds have special bills to eat different kinds of foods. Cardinals, warblers, and pelicans might feed along a forested coastline. Here you would see cardinals crack seeds with their thick bills. You'd see warblers pick out insects from the stems of leaves in trees. You would also see pelicans scoop up fish from the water with their bills that work like nets. In these ways, three kinds of birds survive in one area.

1. ✓**Checkpoint** Give two examples of adaptations and tell how they help an animal survive.

2. 🖉 **Writing in Science Descriptive** There are birds that wade into ponds and spear fish for food. Use library-media center resources to learn about the adaptations that help these birds survive. Write a paragraph.

A small, thin bill helps the warbler pick out insects for food.

Adaptations for Protection

The way an animal looks and acts can help it survive. Some animals protect themselves with body patterns and color that are hard to see. This is called *camouflage*. Other animals have colors or markings that copy those of a poisonous or more dangerous animal. The enemies of these animals leave them alone. Animals may use chemicals to defend themselves. Skunks, for example, spray a bad-smelling liquid at their enemies. Still other animals climb, run, hop, jump, fly, or swim away from danger.

Body parts such as shells, teeth, claws, hooves, bills, or pointed body parts also protect animals from danger. For example, the porcupine is covered in sharp quills. These special hairs have barbs on their tips. When the porcupine senses danger, it uses its muscles to make the quills stand up. Then it turns around and swings its tail. If the porcupine hits an attacker with its tail, the quills can pierce the attacker's skin. The barbs on the quills keep them attached to the attacker.

Porcupines have loose, barbed quills to protect them from their enemies.

Structures That Help Animals Survive

Camouflage	Armor	Copying	Poison
Animals that can harm or be harmed by this crab spider do not notice it.	Spikes and horns protect this horned lizard.	A harmless hover fly looks like a dangerous hornet	Lion fish have poisonous spines.
These harlequin shrimp blend in with the bright sea fans.	This crab sheds its protective shell in order to grow bigger.	A viceroy butterfly looks like a bad-tasting monarch butterfly.	Monarch butterflies taste bad because of the food they eat.
The fur color of this arctic fox changes with the seasons.	A cassowary has a tough helmet to protect its head as it runs through brush.	This king snake looks similar to the deadly coral snake.	Coral snakes bite with venomous fangs.

✔ Lesson Review

1. Give examples of body parts that protect animals from danger.

2. How would tasting bad protect an animal?

3. **Main Idea and Details** Fill in a graphic organizer with the main idea on page 121 and the details that support it.

What are different environments where things live?

Each kind of living thing is adapted for survival in its environment.

Biomes

American bison and African zebras live on different continents. They seem very different, but are similar in one important way. They are adapted for living in large areas of grass. Major areas that have a similar year-round weather pattern and support similar kinds of living things are called a **biome.** The plants and animals living in a biome are adapted to getting what they need in that biome.

A California Biome

One biome can be found on hillsides of much of California. Mild, wet winters and hot, dry summers support *chaparral*. This is a dense layer of evergreen shrubs that grows well in such weather. Thick, waxy leaves keep shrubs from losing water. Fires occur often, fueled by the waxy leaves. The fires' heat opens seeds. Many roots survive the fires. Afterwards, roots and seeds sprout new plants.

Unlike coyotes, bobcats hunt mostly during the day. The only animals that they eat are the ones they hunt.

Coyotes hunt at all hours for desert cottontails, mice, rats, and lizards. They also eat berries, insects, and animals that have died.

Standard Focus 3LS3.a Students know plants and animals have structures that serve different functions in growth, survival, and reproduction. **3LS3.b** Students know examples of diverse life forms in different environments, such as oceans, deserts, tundra, forests, grasslands, and wetlands.

Desert cottontails quietly nibble on leaves and soft bark. Both coyotes and bobcats hunt them. Cottontails are adapted to reproducing more than once a year. Raising many young makes up for losses to the hunters.

Animals That Live In the Chaparral

Desert cottontails hide under the shrubs in the chaparral. Coyotes and bobcats use their fine senses of sight and smell to hunt them. Cottontails run in a zigzag way when alarmed. This helps them avoid getting caught. Coyotes eat more kinds of food than bobcats. Coyotes will also hunt at night. These adaptations allow enough food for both coyotes and bobcats.

1. ✓**Checkpoint** How are coyotes adapted to the chaparral?

2. ✏ **Writing in Science** **Descriptive** Write a newspaper article about the chaparral biome. Describe the kinds of living things visitors see.

The leaves of shrubs in the chaparral have a thick coating. This keeps the shrubs from losing water.

Coniferous Forest
Coniferous tree branches easily shed winter snow. Waxy needles lose little water when cold winds blow.

Rain Forest
Sitka spruce and western hemlock trees are adapted to the cool, wet winters in the rain forest.

Wetland
The salty tides that flow into coastal wetlands supply nutrients. Many living things find food in the mud.

Chaparral
Evergreen shrubs grow well during mild, wet winters and hot, dry summers. Fires spread quickly and often.

Ocean
Forests of giant kelp grow in the waters off the West Coast. These algae support a lot of sea life.

Desert
The roots of many desert plants spread out over a large area. This helps the plants get water from a dry environment.

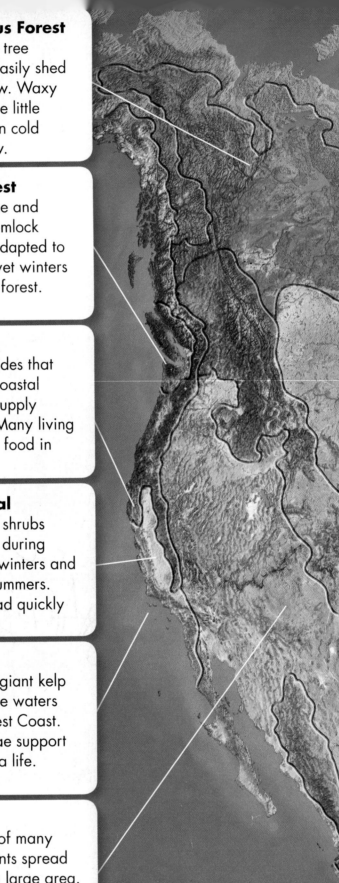

Tundra
The ground is too frozen and dry to support the roots of trees. Snow protects grasses and sedges from cold winds.

Grassland
There is enough rain to support many kinds of grasses and flowering plants, but few trees.

Deciduous Forest
Rain that falls mostly during the warm summers helps this forest grow. Trees shed their leaves before the cold, snowy winter.

Biomes of North America

Several biomes are found in North America. Each biome covers a large area. Plants provide the basis for life in each biome. This is because plants supply most of the food energy. Many biomes are named after the important kinds of plants that grow in them.

✓ Lesson Review

1. Why are trees common in a rain forest biome but not in a tundra biome?

2. Would a plant adapted to a deciduous forest grow well in a desert? Explain your answer.

3. **Main Idea and Details** Fill in a graphic organizer with the main idea on this page and the details that support it.

127

How do living things survive in places with few trees?

Many kinds of plants and animals live in grassland, desert, and tundra biomes, but few trees do.

Grasslands

Think about looking out over a wide, grassy field. The tops of the grasses sway as a summer breeze blows through. A **grassland** is a biome that has many grasses and flowering plants but few trees. Grasslands have cold winters and hot, dry summers. Because the area receives little rain, the soil is dry. Trees cannot grow well in this soil. They need more water.

Grasses, such as Indian grass and little bluestem, grow well here. Grassland plants grow roots deep into the ground. This adaptation helps the plants in many ways. When grazing animals, fire, or cold winters kill the plants above ground, the roots survive. The roots store food for the new growth in the spring. Deep roots also help the plants get water in the dry, hot summers.

Winters can be cold in the grasslands. Deep roots help the plants store food for the next growing season.

This deep-rooted blazing star is a grassland plant with pretty flowers. Flowers attract insects that help the plant make seeds.

Standard Focus 3LS3.a Students know plants and animals have structures that serve different functions in growth, survival, and reproduction.
3LS3.b Students know examples of diverse life forms in different environments, such as oceans, deserts, tundra, forests, grasslands, and wetlands.

Huge herds of bison once roamed the grasslands. Bison have teeth and stomachs that are adapted for eating tough grass.

Grasshoppers use their long legs to climb and jump. Their mouthparts are adapted to chew grass. They use wings to fly to different grass plants.

1. ✓**Checkpoint** What is a grassland?

2. **Main Idea and Details** Fill in a graphic organizer with the main idea of the last paragraph on page 128 and the details that support it.

Desert

A **desert** is a biome that gets very little rain. Days are often hot, but the nights are cool or even cold. Many people think of deserts as just sand and rock. However, desert biomes can be full of life.

A cactus is a plant with adaptations for life in a desert. A cactus makes food in its stem, not its leaves. Stems lose less water than leaves do. When it does rain, some cactus stems expand to store water for later use. A waxy covering keeps them from losing water. The leaves of many cactus plants are sharp spines. Instead of making food, the leaves protect the cactus from thirsty animals and direct sunlight.

More water makes stem walls swell outward.

Water from roots is stored in this area.

The stem of a cactus expands as it stores water. It shrinks as the cactus uses water.

Water from roots passes up these tubes.

The spines on this cactus are a special kind of leaf.

Many desert animals rest out of sight during the hottest time of day. For example, the kangaroo rat stays in a cool, moist den. At night, it comes out of its hiding place. The dark night protects it from animals that hunt it. Certain desert snakes, however, can locate it by the heat it gives off.

Like desert plants, desert animals must conserve the small amount of water they find. Kangaroo rats get water from the foods they eat. They almost never have to drink water. Their wastes are very dry because their bodies absorb as much water as possible.

The kangaroo rat gets water from the seeds it eats. It can store extra food in a pouch inside its cheeks.

1. ✓**Checkpoint** How is a cactus adapted to life in a desert biome?

2. **Writing in Science** **Descriptive** Death Valley National Park, California, protects one of the hottest, driest deserts on Earth. Use materials from a library-media center to describe plants and animals found there.

Map Fact

Joshua Tree National Park is in a desert in southern California. Joshua trees are a kind of yucca plant.

Tundra

The **tundra** is a cold, dry biome located in the most northern part of the world and on high mountains. Parts of Alaska and Canada are tundra. Winters there are long and cold. Cold winds blow the little snow that falls. Summers are short and cool. The snow melts in summer, but the soil below the surface stays frozen all year.

Summer daylight lasts a long time in the tundra. In some places, the summer Sun shines 24 hours a day. Winter daylight hours are very few. Some places get no sunlight in winter.

Survival In the Tundra

Most plants and animals would not survive in the tundra. Few trees grow. Their roots cannot grow into the frozen soil. Grasses and small plants grow here instead. These plants grow close to the ground under the snow. This protects them from the tundra's strong winter winds.

In summer, melting snow forms ponds in the tundra. Ducks, geese, and swans nest near these ponds. Many birds feed on the many insects that hatch in the tundra in spring and summer. Most of these birds travel to warmer places during the winter. Some, such as snow geese, fly long distances to find food and raise young.

An Arctic gray wolf's fur keeps it warm in the cold tundra. These animals work together in packs to hunt caribou. They tear the food they capture with sharp teeth.

Trees do not grow in this tundra.

Lichen can survive cold, wind, and snow. They get water from the water vapor in the air.

Caribou travel in large herds to protect themselves from animals that hunt them. In winter, they find food by digging through the snow with their front hooves.

✓ **Lesson Review**

1. Why do most tundra plants grow close to the ground?

2. What adaptations help caribou survive?

TARGET SKILL
3. **Main Idea and Details** Fill in a graphic organizer with the main idea of Survival in the Tundra on page 132 and the details that support it.

133

How do living things survive in forests?

Forest biomes support kinds of plants and animals not found in other biomes.

Pine, spruce, fir, and hemlock trees are kinds of trees that grow in coniferous forests.

Coniferous Forests

Coniferous forests grow well where a lot of snow falls, and winds blow cold and dry. Tree branches easily bend downward. The weight of snow does not break them. Most coniferous trees keep their leaves in winter. The leaves are narrow and lose little water in the cold winds. Tree leaves are ready to make food when spring arrives. Leaves in the shape of needles can gather sunlight from many directions.

Standard Focus 3LS3.a Students know plants and animals have structures that serve different functions in growth, survival, and reproduction.
3LS3.b Students know examples of diverse life forms in different environments, such as oceans, deserts, tundra, forests, grasslands, and wetlands.

Woodpeckers use their chisel-shaped bills to hammer holes into bark. They use their long tongues to probe the holes for insects.

Deciduous Forests

Trees in *deciduous* forests grow during the warm spring and summer when it rains. They shed their leaves in the fall. This adaptation allows the trees to save energy during cold, snowy winters. Shrubs and other plants grow beneath the trees.

Animals are adapted to using the trees for shelter and food. Birds and squirrels build nests in them for raising young. Trees grow nuts, acorns, and fruit that birds, squirrels, and bears eat.

Oak, maple, and beech trees grow in deciduous forests.

Black bears use their claws to dig for insects and climb trees to find nuts and acorns. They also dig dens in which to spend the winter and give birth to cubs.

1. ✓**Checkpoint** How are coniferous forests and deciduous forests alike? How do they differ?

2. ✏ **Writing in Science Descriptive** Suppose you are walking through a deciduous forest. Describe what you might see, hear, and touch.

Rain Forest Plants

One kind of rain forest exists in places with mild temperatures and lots of winter rain. Coniferous trees grow tall in this biome. Their leaves capture sunlight high above the dim forest floor.

The tall trees block most sunlight from reaching the ground. The ground is covered with branches and dead trees. Many small plants called moss form a soft, green carpet. Mushrooms are parts of fungi that live in and on the wood of dead trees. Fungi can break down the dead wood and use it for food.

Rain Forest Animals

Flying squirrels are adapted to the rain forest. So are the spotted owls that hunt them. The squirrels save energy by gliding over the jumbled forest floor as they look for mushrooms to eat. Spotted owls see well in the dim forest as they hunt the squirrels. An owl's flight feathers make very little sound. The owl grasps a squirrel with sharp talons. It carries the meal to its nest. Thick branches surround the nest and protect it from great horned owls that hunt the spotted owl.

Elk use their antlers to defend themselves.

Map Fact

Rain forests grow in such places as the western slopes of the Olympic Mountains in the state of Washington. Here temperatures are mild. Winter rainfall can be as much as 400 cm. Sitka spruce and western hemlocks fill the forests.

Spotted owls see well during dark nights of hunting in the rain forest.

This flying squirrel is able to glide through the forest.

This dead log is a good food source for these fungi.

✔ **Lesson Review**

1. How does growing very tall help conifers in a rain forest?

2. What adaptations help a spotted owl survive?

3. **Main Idea and Details** Fill in a graphic organizer with the main idea of Rain Forest Animals on page 136 and the details that support it.

How do living things survive in water environments?

Some plants and animals live in fresh water, others live in salt water. Still others live in a mixture of both fresh and salt water.

Wetlands

Squish! The mucky ground in a wetland would get your feet wet in a hurry! A **wetland** is a low area that is covered by water for at least part of the year. Water brings in nutrients, which help plants to grow.

There are different kinds of wetlands. Coastal wetlands like the one pictured are salty. Salt water from the ocean flows in with the tides. Some living things can live in salty environments. Others cannot. The different amounts of salt cause different kinds of plants and animals to live along the wetland.

This shorebird's long legs and bill help it find food in the salt marsh.

Living in Mud

Many tiny living things are at home in the mud of a salt marsh. Most of them grow from eating dead plant material mixed in with the mud. Crabs, shrimps, and snails feed on these creatures. The tides also carry worms and clams into the salt marsh. It's hard to see, but the mud in a salt marsh is filled with life!

Standard Focus 3LS3.a Students know plants and animals have structures that serve different functions in growth, survival, and reproduction.
3LS3.b Students know examples of diverse life forms in different environments, such as oceans, deserts, tundra, forests, grasslands, and wetlands.

Many kinds of birds feed on small creatures that live in marshes. Long-legged shorebirds can wade through the shallow water of marshes without sinking. Their feet are adapted to keep them upright in the mud. They use their long, thin bills to dig through the mud for food.

Map Fact

This salt marsh is in Point Reyes National Seashore on the coast of northern California. Such wetlands are home for many kinds of wildlife.

1. ✓**Checkpoint** Why are there so many living things in the mud of most wetlands?

2. ✏ **Writing in Science Formal Letter** Write a letter to community leaders about wetlands. Explain how wetlands are important places for wildlife and should be protected.

Many animals that live in the water breathe with gills. The gills are behind the slits, which appear on the side of this shark. Gills take in oxygen from the water.

A hard outer shell protects and supports the crab's body. As the animal grows, it molts, or sheds, its shell and grows a larger one.

Unlike fish, whales have lungs for breathing air. A layer of fat called blubber lies beneath the whale's smooth skin and keeps the animal warm.

A cuttlefish can move fast by squirting a jet of water out of its body. This adaptation helps it escape from its enemies.

Kelp forests off the coast of California are home to sea otters, fish, and other animals adapted to the ocean.

Oceans

Oceans are biomes that cover much of Earth's surface. Ocean water contains salt. The ocean is shallow along the shore. Clams, crabs, algae, fish, and coral live close to the shore. Seabirds fly over the water and scoop or dive to get food.

In deeper water, algae called kelp form underwater forests. Gas-filled "floats" keep the algae upright and closer to light. These kelp forests are home to many different animals, especially fish. Fish use gills to get the oxygen they need from water. They have sleek bodies that allow them to move quickly through the water.

Whales, sea lions, and sea otters also live in the ocean. They do not have gills and must come to the surface to breathe air. Their bodies are adapted for moving swiftly through water. Since fur would slow them down, sea lions have very short hair. Whales have almost no hair at all. Sea otters have thick, oily fur that keeps them warm.

✓ Lesson Review

1. How are kelp adapted for holding themselves up in the water?

2. How are whales adapted to live and move in cold ocean waters?

3. **Main Idea and Details** Fill in a graphic organizer with the main idea of Oceans on this page and the details that support it.

Math in Science

Comparing Data

The major grasslands of North America are located in six areas, as shown on the map. The tall-grass prairie, the mixed-grass prairie, and the short-grass prairie together are known as the Central Prairies.

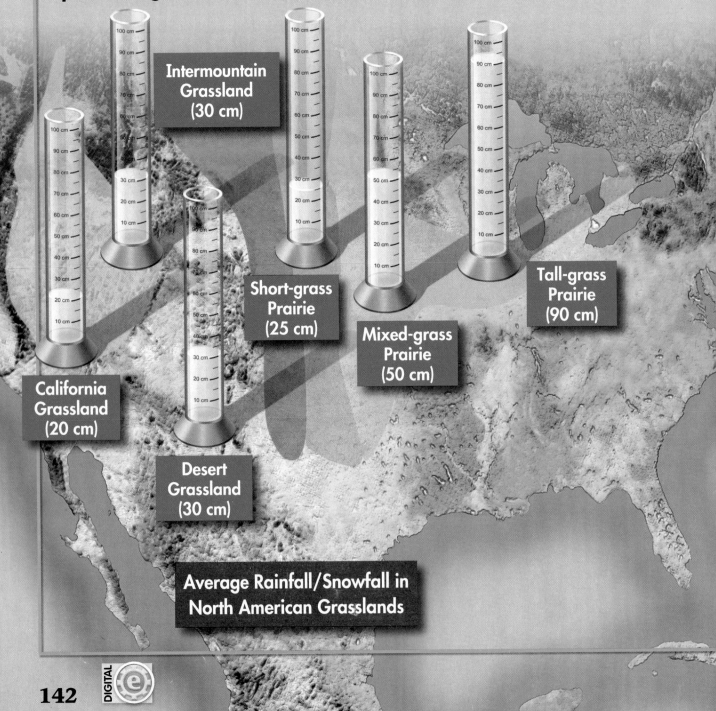

Intermountain Grassland (30 cm)

California Grassland (20 cm)

Desert Grassland (30 cm)

Short-grass Prairie (25 cm)

Mixed-grass Prairie (50 cm)

Tall-grass Prairie (90 cm)

Average Rainfall/Snowfall in North American Grasslands

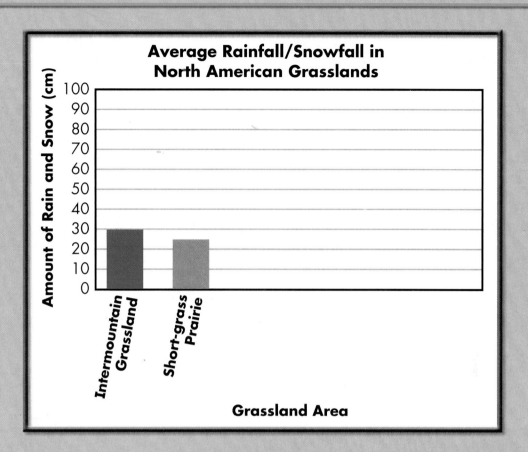

Average Rainfall/Snowfall in North American Grasslands

Amount of Rain and Snow (cm)

Grassland Area

Use the map and the graph to answer each question.

1 Copy the bar graph on grid paper and complete it. Your graph should show the data for all six grasslands.

2 Which describes how the amount of rain and snow in the Central Prairies changes?

A. increases from west to east   B. decreases from west to east

C. increases from north to south   D. decreases from north to south

3 Which grassland gets the most rain and snow? Which gets the least?

Lab zone Take-Home Activity

Find out about rainfall and snowfall amounts in a biome in North America. Show the data on a bar graph.

Investigate How do some desert plants change when they store water?

Materials

construction paper

masking tape

plastic bag

water

tape measure or paper ruler

Process Skills

After you **collect data** you can use it to help describe and compare objects, events, and **measurements.**

What to Do

① Fold the paper.

② Tape the ends to **make a model** of a cactus.

③ Put the plastic bag inside.

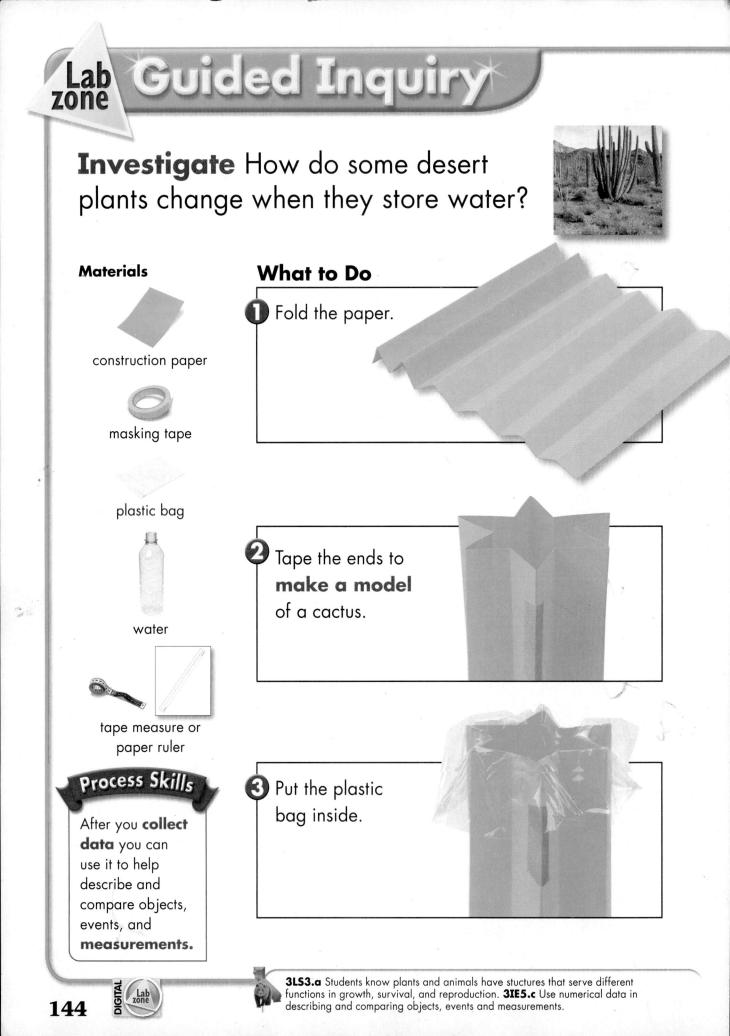

144 DIGITAL Lab zone

3LS3.a Students know plants and animals have stuctures that serve different functions in growth, survival, and reproduction. **3IE5.c** Use numerical data in describing and comparing objects, events, and measurements.

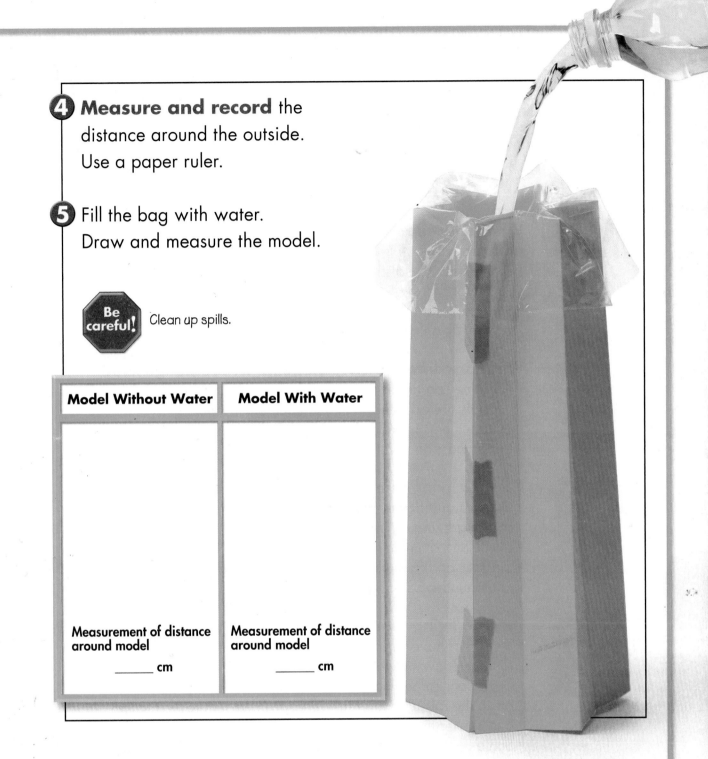

4 **Measure and record** the distance around the outside. Use a paper ruler.

5 Fill the bag with water. Draw and measure the model.

Be careful! Clean up spills.

Model Without Water	Model With Water
Measurement of distance around model _____ cm	Measurement of distance around model _____ cm

Explain Your Results

1. Describe and compare your model before and after adding water. Look at your **data.** How did your **measurement** change?

2. How might storing water help a plant survive in the desert?

Go Further

A fat cactus stores more water than a thin cactus. How could you make a model to show this?

Chapter 4 Reviewing Key Concepts

Each kind of plant and animal has adaptations that help it survive in a particular habitat or biome.

Lesson 1

What structures help plants and animals live and grow?
- Plants and animals need food, air, water, and space to live and grow.
- An adaptation is a structure or ability that helps a plant or animal meet its needs.

Lesson 2

What are different environments where things live?
- A biome is a major type of environment. Plants and animals are adapted to live in each environment.
- Environments include oceans, deserts, tundra, forests, grasslands, and wetlands. Chaparral is found in California.

Lesson 3

How do living things survive in places with few trees?
- Grasses and flowering plants in grasslands have deep roots. Large, grazing animals live in grasslands.
- Plants and animals that can survive with little water live in deserts.
- Grasses and flowers in the tundra have shallow roots. Animals in the tundra can survive long, cold winters.

Lesson 4

How do living things survive in forests?
- Trees that have needle-shaped leaves and animals adapted to cold, snowy winters live in coniferous forests.
- Deciduous forests have trees with broad, flat leaves that drop off in the fall. Animals that depend on these trees for food and shelter live there too.
- Some plants and animals can survive in the shade of cool, wet rain forests.

Lesson 5

How do living things survive in water environments?
- Plants and animals that can survive in a muddy environment live in wetlands.
- Some algae can live in the ocean. Many animals in the ocean use gills or lungs to get oxygen.

Cross-Curricular Links

English–Language Arts

Building Vocabulary

Look back on page 114. Look at the picture behind the word *adaptation*. Write a paragraph that explains how the word is related to the picture.

Mathematics

Desert Heat

Furnace Creek is in a desert biome. The average high temperature in July is 115°F. The average low temperature is 88°F. What is the difference between the average high and average low temperatures?

Visual and Performing Arts

Adaptation Art

A black bear is a large, furry animal. It has claws and can climb trees. It also has teeth which help it eat both plants and animals. Draw a picture of this animal. Label the adaptations that help the animal get what it needs to live.

Challenge!

English–Language Arts

Biome

Choose a biome found in North America. Use the library-media center to locate it on a map. Describe the adaptations of the plants and animals in this biome.

Chapter 4 Review/Test

Vocabulary

adaptation (page 120)	**grassland** (page 128)
biome (page 124)	**tundra** (page 132)
desert (page 130)	**wetland** (page 138)

Fill in the blanks with the correct vocabulary words. If you have trouble, read the listed page again.

1. A(n) _____ gets little rain.

2. A low area covered by water for part of the year is a(n) _____.

3. A(n) _____ is a body part or ability that helps a living thing meet its needs.

4. A major type of environment that has distinctive year-round weather is a(n) _____.

5. _____ is cold, dry, and has frozen ground.

6. A(n) _____ has grasses with deep roots but few trees.

Think About It

7. Why do some cactus make food in stems and not in leaves?

8. How are some plants in the chaparral adapted to fire?

9. How does looking like a poisonous animal help some animals survive?

10. **Process Skills** **Interpret Data** Look at the data in the chart. What biome is described? Explain your answer.

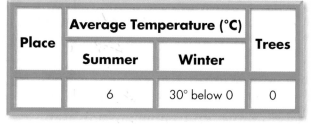

| Place | Average Temperature (°C) | | Trees |
	Summer	Winter	
	6	30° below 0	0

11. **Main Idea and Details** Make a graphic organizer like the one below. Fill in the main idea that the details support.

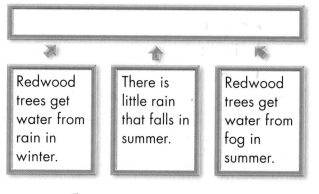

Redwood trees get water from rain in winter.

There is little rain that falls in summer.

Redwood trees get water from fog in summer.

12. **Writing in Science** **Descriptive** Describe the adaptations of plants and animals that live in the ocean.

California Standards Practice

Write the letter of the correct answer.

13. What kind of bill would a bird that eats mainly seeds have?

A a bill with a hanging pouch

B a small, thin bill

C a long, curved bill

D a short, strong bill

14. What do shorebirds suited for life in a wetland have?

A stems that swell outward

B gills and chisel-shaped bills

C long legs and long, thin bills

D thick legs and sharp talons

15. Which is an adaptation that helps whales survive?

A squirting a jet of water

B hard outer shell

C oily hairs

D a layer of fat called blubber

16. In which biome would you probably find trees with needle-shaped leaves?

A coniferous forest

B deciduous forest

C grassland

D tundra

17. How do claws help black bears?

A to dig for insects

B to dive for fish

C to make food

D to crack open seeds

18. Plant roots in grasslands

A draw up water in winter.

B are eaten by grazing animals.

C store food.

D die when fire burns the grasses.

19. A cactus stores water in its

A flowers.

B stem.

C leaves.

D spines.

20. Pictured are plants that live in what biome?

A chaparral

B tundra

C grassland

D coniferous forest

Eric Stolen

Eric Stolen

"Getting wet, dirty, hot, bug-bitten and chased by critters" are things Eric Stolen loves.

Eric Stolen is a wildlife biologist at NASA's Kennedy Space Center, which includes a wildlife refuge. Mr. Stolen studies how wading birds choose a place to live and how they get food.

Mr. Stolen finds ways to study the birds without them noticing he is there. Sometimes he wades through mud. Other times he flies over the birds in a helicopter. Mr. Stolen uses binoculars and other tools to see what the birds are doing.

When Eric was growing up, he often went camping, hiking, and boating. He became interested in nature and animals while he was in grade school. Later on, Mr. Stolen studied biology in college. He never tires of studying nature because there are so many new and interesting things to see and learn.

Lab zone Take-Home Activity

Spend an hour outdoors. Find a place where you can see birds or other animals. Write a paragraph about the animals you see and what they do.

Chapter 5

Living Things in a World of Change

Standards Focus Questions

- How do living things change environments?
- How do changes in the environment affect living things?
- How do living things compare to those of long ago?

How does change affect the survival of living things?

competition

habitat

Chapter 5 Vocabulary

extinct

fossil

153

Explore What can happen when an environment changes?

Make a model of a wetland environment. Investigate what happens to the plants when the environment changes.

Materials

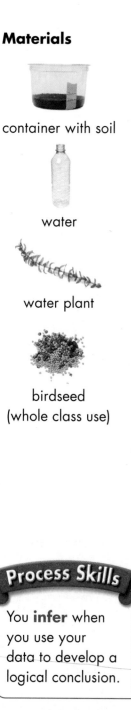

container with soil

water

water plant

birdseed
(whole class use)

What to Do

1 Pour water in the container up to the 3 cm mark. Allow the contents to settle overnight.

2 Place a water plant in the container. Put the container in a warm place with bright light.

3 Every other day, add 4 seeds.

4 **Observe** and record how the model environment changes.

Explain Your Results

1. What changes did you observe in the model environment?

2. **Infer** If you added water daily how might the results have been different?

3LS3.d Students know when the environment changes, some plants and animals survive and reproduce; others die or move to new locations. **3IE5.e** Collect data in an investigation and analyze those data to develop a logical conclusion.

DIGITAL Lab zone

How to Read Science

Make Inferences

As you read, you put facts together to develop new ideas. You **make inferences** when you do this. Facts you use to make an inference can come from:

- what you already know about the topic of the reading
- facts given in the reading
- your own experiences.

The story below presents facts about cutting trees.

Newspaper story

Forest Fragments

Areas of forest that remain after trees are cut for lumber are called fragments. Many forest animals moving between forest fragments don't survive. Winds blow down trees along fragment edges.

Apply It!

Make a graphic organizer like the one shown. Fill it in with three facts from the story above. Then write an **inference** about the health of forest fragments.

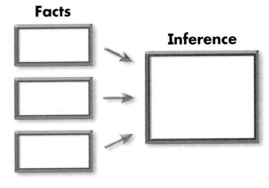

Facts

Inference

You Are There!

You're walking along a trail in the cool rain forest. You step onto fallen branches covered in soft moss but make no sound. It's rather dark in this forest! Wait. What is that open area in the light? Why are those young trees crowded together on that fallen log? Is this the way a younger forest replaces an older one?

DIGITAL

How do living things change their environment?

As living things get what they need from their environments, they often change those environments.

Changing the Environment

A **habitat** is where a living thing makes its home. A habitat provides the resources a plant or animal needs to survive and grow.

A habitat is like a balance. One side holds what lives in the habitat. The other side holds resources the habitat provides. If the habitat provides enough resources to support life, the balance is level.

Change often tips the balance. For example, tree seeds may sprout on a log and start to grow a new forest. The young trees need light and growing room. When two or more living things need the same resources in order to survive, they are in **competition.** The young trees are in competition. Some trees get enough light. As their branches grow, they shade nearby plants. The habitat changes. Other young trees may not get enough light to survive.

1. **✓ Checkpoint** When does competition happen?

2. **Make Inferences** Tree tops grow close together. Use a graphic organizer to infer what may happen between young trees that grow at ground level.

keyword:
habitat
code:
gr3p157

Beavers Causing Change

Some animals change the environment to improve their habitat. Beavers, for example, need deep water. If the stream where they live is too shallow, the beavers build a pond. They cut down trees with their teeth. They use the wood to build a dam across the stream. The blocked water forms a pond behind the dam.

The change helps plants and animals that need to live in still water. Also, the trees the beavers cut down no longer shade the ground below. Small plants and shrubs that benefit from direct sunlight grow in their place.

The change harms plants and animals whose homes are flooded. Trees needed to make the dam are lost. The pond also takes homes away from plants and animals that prefer the flowing water of streams.

Beavers change the environment when they build their homes and dams of sticks and mud.

This place was once a grassy meadow. How has this beaver dam changed it?

People have built homes and farms in this environment. Did the change help or harm plants and animals that first lived there?

Humans Causing Change

People need resources just as other living things do. When people build homes, they change the environment. They cut down forests and plow up grasslands to make room for houses and farms. Each of these changes affects the environment.

Sometimes animals and humans compete for space. People move to places where animals live. Then they might find coyotes in their backyards or a deer strolling onto the lanes of a busy highway.

1. ✓**Checkpoint** Describe how beavers change their environment. Then tell how each change helps or harms other living things.

2. ✎**Writing in Science Descriptive**
Like beavers, humans build dams that block rivers. Use the library-media center to find out how dams change the environment. Write a paragraph about what you learn.

Plants and Algae Causing Change

Changes can help some living things and harm others. For example, purple loosestrife was brought to the United States. No animals eat this plant. It is spreading to new places. That's great for the loosestrife! But there is less space for other plants to grow. Some kinds are pushed out entirely.

Fertilizer put on fields helps crops grow. Rainwater can wash some fertilizer from fields into streams and lakes where tiny algae live. Then the fertilizer helps the algae grow. If they grow too much, some of the algae block sunlight. Algae that don't get sunlight die. Next, tiny living things that eat dead algae grow in number. This uses up oxygen in the water that fish need to survive. Finally, the fish have to move to a new habitat or die.

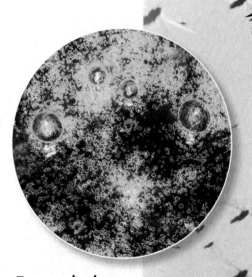

Purple loosestrife competes with other plants for living space.

Too much algae can lead to too little oxygen that fish need.

A Pattern of Change

Some changes repeat in a *cycle*. For example, small mammals called lemmings eat tundra plants. When there is plenty of food, the number of lemmings goes up. Soon, less food is available because the lemmings are eating it. Many leave or die, and the number of lemmings goes down. The grass grows back. The number of lemmings goes up again.

Lemmings cause changes that repeat in a cycle.

Insects Causing Change

These grasshoppers are changing the environment. First, many grasshopper eggs hatch all at once. If there is not enough food to eat, the grasshoppers collect together. Then they travel in a huge swarm to find food. Finally, the swarm destroys plants over a wide area.

✓ Lesson Review

1. Describe helpful changes that living things cause.

2. Describe harmful changes that living things cause.

3. **Writing in Science Narrative** Write a letter to a friend about a swarm of locusts. Tell what happens as they look for food. Describe how they change the environment.

Lesson 2

How do changes in the environment affect living things?

Natural events can change an environment. Some plants and animals survive and reproduce. Others die or move away.

Places with water can dry out during dry seasons. Some plants can live with less water. Others die. Some animals survive. Others die or move away.

Too Little Water

Periods of dry weather change environments. Plants die without water. Animals die or move away.

People can also cause dry conditions when they take water from lakes and streams for farms and homes. The lakes and streams may become too dry for plants to survive and reproduce. Animals die or move to new locations.

Standard Focus 3LS3.d Students know when the environment changes, some plants and animals survive and reproduce; others die or move to new locations.

Many places have become drier over thousands of years. Shrubs and grasses that are adapted to less water replace trees that need more water. Animals that use shrubs and grasses for homes and food replace animals that use trees.

Too Much Water

Living things need water, but too much water all at once can change an environment. Storms can cause floods, which wash away plants, soil, and animals' homes. Floods spread thick blankets of mud. Animals may die, survive, or move to new locations.

The Mississippi River floods often. The floodwaters can carry seeds and mud that is rich in nutrients to new places.

1. ✓**Checkpoint** How do plants and animals change in places that turn drier over thousands of years?

2. 🖉 **Writing** in **Science** **Formal Letter**
Write a letter urging people who live in dry places to use less water in order to protect water resources.

Water is hard to find in the dry season.

Volcanic Eruption

On May 18, 1980, the volcano Mt. St. Helens erupted in the state of Washington. This eruption was huge. One side of the mountain collapsed and slid away. Hot rocks and gases from the volcano quickly melted snow and ice. The water flooded the nearby area. The daytime sky grew dark as the volcano released a cloud of ash into the air. Winds carried the ash around the world.

The blast changed the environment. Rivers of mud covered whole areas. Ash was piled up a meter thick in some places. Large areas of forest that once covered Mt. St. Helens were destroyed.

Very few plants survived the eruption.

Mt. St. Helens erupts and throws tons of ash into the sky.

DIGITAL
Look for Active Art animations at www.pearsonsuccessnet.com

After the Eruption

Plant roots and shrubs covered by snow survived the eruption. Seeds in the soil and those carried by wind sprouted and grew. Once plants grew, animals that need those plants for food could live there too.

Animals that lived underground also survived. Ants, spiders, mice, and gophers were protected from the blast. Birds returned to live in the dead trees left standing. Mice, shrews, and voles then made new homes on the mountain. These attracted weasels and hawks. Even large elk returned.

Each new change has allowed different kinds of plants and the animals that depend on them to live there. The environment won't be the same as it was for a long time. But the mountain is filled with life once more...until the next eruption!

1. **✔ Checkpoint** How were some plants able to survive the eruption of Mt. St. Helens?

2. **Make Inferences** After Mt. St. Helens erupted, why did more plants have to grow before more animals could move in? Use a graphic organizer.

New plants begin to grow after the eruption. They attract animals that use them for food and habitat.

Wildfire

Zap! Lightning strikes a tree in a forest, setting it ablaze. Soon a wildfire races through the forest out of control. Trees with thick bark survive. Others burn. Dead brush and small plants burn away. Sometimes very large areas go up in smoke. A fire brings a major change to the forest.

Before a fire, a forest is often crowded with trees and other plants.

The temperature of a forest fire can reach 800°C.

After the Fire

Fire kills trees and destroys animal homes. Fires that are not severe, however, can be helpful. They clear the forest of dead wood. Surviving trees have more living space. Burnt ash makes soil healthy. Plants that need more sunlight can grow. Fires often create habitat for more kinds of plants and animals.

A forest that has burnt to the ground goes through many changes. Animals that hunt enter the burnt forest. They find food easily because other animals have fewer places to hide. Birds that eat seeds spot them easily. Wind and animals carry in new seeds. Grasses, flowers, and shrubs adapted to strong sunlight grow. The changes they bring set the stage for the next group of plants. A habitat for trees develops. In time, the forest grows back.

This young tree has plenty of living space and sunlight.

Fire has cleared this forest for new growth.

✓ Lesson Review

1. How can a fire help living things?

2. Why are animals that hunt other animals the first to enter a burned forest?

3. **Make Inferences** Infer why grasses and shrubs often grow before trees do after a forest has burnt to the ground. Use a graphic organizer.

How do living things compare to those of long ago?

Fossils show how plants and animals alive today compare to those that lived long ago. Fossils also show how the environment has changed.

Fossils

An environment may change more quickly than a kind of plant or animal can adapt. The change may cause these kinds of plants or animals to disappear, or go extinct. A kind of plant or animal that is **extinct** no longer lives on Earth.

Most living things have become extinct over Earth's history. We can't observe them, since they no longer exist. But we can study the fossils they left behind. A **fossil** is the remains or mark of a living thing from long ago.

The fern that made this fossil lived about 350 million years ago.

What Fossils Show

Fossils hold clues about extinct plants and animals and their environments. We know that some extinct animals looked like animals that are alive today. We know that others looked different. We also know ways their environments have changed.

Many extinct ferns looked like this fern growing in Redwood National Park in California.

Standard Focus 3LS3.e Students know that some kinds of organisms that once lived on Earth have completely disappeared and that some of those resembled others that are alive today.

This 125-million-year-old dinosaur fossil looks like an alligator. Modern alligators live in warm, wet areas. The dinosaur's habitat was probably similar.

This is a fossil of an extinct flying animal. It may have flown like the one in the big picture on the left.

This is a model of an extinct flying animal. Skin stretched between a leg and a long finger on each arm helped the animal to fly. Teeth helped it to grasp fish.

1. ✓ **Checkpoint** What can we learn from fossils?

2. ✏️ **Writing in Science**
Description Describe the fossil in the middle of this page. How do its features support its likeness to the animal in the big picture?

169

Changes in Plants over Time

We see from plant fossils that the first plants did not have flowers or cones. Many were like today's ferns. As Earth changed over time, however, plants changed too. Trees that made cones appeared. Then plants with flowers appeared. Many of these kinds of plants have since completely disappeared.

Magnolias are an example of a group of flowering plants that has survived. The world was warm and wet year-round when magnolias first appeared. Dinosaurs were everywhere. Magnolia trees grew thick leaves that they kept year-round. The period during which creamy white flowers blossomed lasted for months. Magnolias just like this are alive today.

As environments changed, so did the magnolias. Some places now have cold winters. Many magnolias are adapted to cold weather. They lose their leaves in fall. Their flowers blossom all at once before the leaves appear in the spring. Even so, they are similar to those of magnolias that lived long ago. The flower of the magnolia has remained unchanged for 100 million years.

Fossils of magnolia leaves from long ago look similar to today's magnolia leaves.

Flowers of deciduous magnolias blossom all at once in the spring. After flowering, the trees grow new leaves for the summer.

170

The first magnolia trees were similar to many magnolias alive today. The feathered dinosaur is extinct.

1. ✓**Checkpoint** How have some magnolias changed over time? How have these magnolias stayed the same?

2. **Make Inferences** Fossil magnolia leaves come from a tree that kept its leaves year-round. Magnolias still grow in the area where the fossils were found. They lose their leaves in the fall. Use a graphic organizer to help explain this difference.

Changes in Animals over Time

We can use fossils to learn how animals and the environments they lived in have changed over time. For instance, you can compare the teeth of extinct animals to those of animals today. Teeth give clues about what the extinct animals ate. Animals that eat meat have cutting and tearing teeth. Animals that eat plants have grinding teeth. If fossils of plant-eating animals are found, perhaps many plants grew in the area.

Suppose the *Tyrannosaurus rex* fossil on this page was found in the desert-like Badlands of South Dakota. The dinosaur's sharp teeth may mean it tore off and swallowed meat from other animals.

Fossils of trees that lived in swamps have been found in the Badlands. Scientists have also found large plant-eating dinosaurs. *T. rex* may have hunted them. These fossils show that the Badlands were once in a warm, wet area. The area has since become very dry with few plants.

Today the Badlands in South Dakota are almost a desert. Only animals adapted to a hot, dry environment can live there.

This collared lizard is a tiny, modern-day reptile. It resembles dinosaurs of long ago and may or may not be related.

Dinosaurs like this *T. rex* became extinct about 65 million years ago.

Millions of years ago the Badlands were warm and wet year-round. This picture shows how the habitat of this T. rex might have looked at that time.

✓ Lesson Review

1. How can we learn about extinct plants and animals?

2. How can scientists use animal fossils to learn about what extinct animals ate?

3. **Make Inferences** The fossil of a very large plant-eating dinosaur is found in a desert. Use a graphic organizer to infer what the dinosaur's environment was once like.

173

Graphing Change Over Time

Scientists sometimes conduct studies on how the size of a certain group of plants or animals changes over a period of time. You can see an example in the line graph below. It shows changes in a group of rabbits in a California park. The graph shows how the size of a rabbit group changed over a 10-year period.

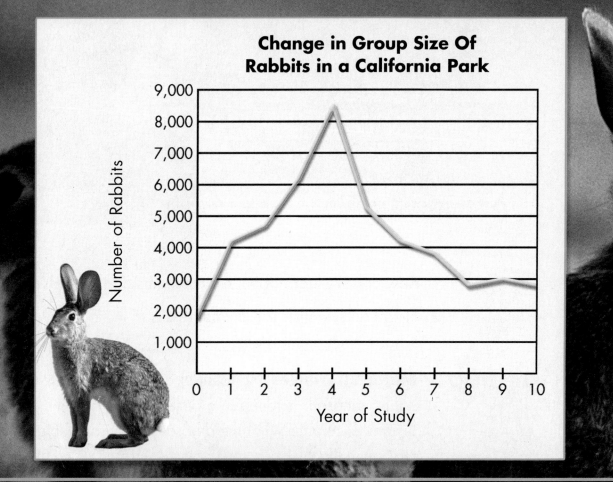

Change in Group Size Of Rabbits in a California Park

Number of Rabbits

Year of Study

DIGITAL

Use the graph on page 174 to answer the following questions.

1. During which group of years did the population of rabbits increase each year?
   A. year 0 to year 4
   B. year 0 to year 5
   C. year 4 to year 7
   D. year 7 to year 10

2. What was the size of the group in year 9?
   A. 9
   B. 3,000
   C. 9,000
   D. 3,500

3. During which group of years did the number of rabbits decrease each year?
   A. year 2 to year 4
   B. year 3 to year 5
   C. year 4 to year 8
   D. year 8 to year 10

4. What are some possible reasons for the decrease in the number of rabbits?

Lab zone Take-Home Activity

Find data about changes in the number of people in your city or state over the last 10 years. Display your results in a line graph like the one on page 174.

175

Investigate What can happen to plants when the environment changes?

Changes in the environment can affect which plants can grow in a place. Irrigation has led to a buildup of salt in the soil in some farming areas. In these places some plants can no longer grow.

Materials

paper cups

pencil

plastic spoon

potting soil

30 radish seeds

tap water

salty water

very salty water

What to Do

1 Use a pencil to make 3 small holes in the bottom of each cup. Use a spoon to fill the cups $\frac{2}{3}$ full of soil.

2 Place 10 radish seeds on top of the potting soil in each cup. Add a thin layer of soil.

Label the cups.

A

B

C

3 Add 5 spoonfuls of water to each cup. Use tap water in cup A. Use salty water in cup B. Use very salty water in cup C. Every day put 1 spoonful of water into each cup.

Put the cups in a bright place.

A

Process Skills

When you record information you have **observed,** you are **collecting data.**

3LS3.d Students know when the environment changes, some plants and animals survive and reproduce; others die or move to new locations. **3IE5.c** Use numerical data in describing and comparing objects, events, and measurements. **3IE5.e** Collect data in an investigation and analyze those data to develop a logical conclusion. (Also **3IE5.0**)

4 **Observe** the cups every day for 10 days.

5 **Collect data.** Each day record how many radish plants are in each cup.

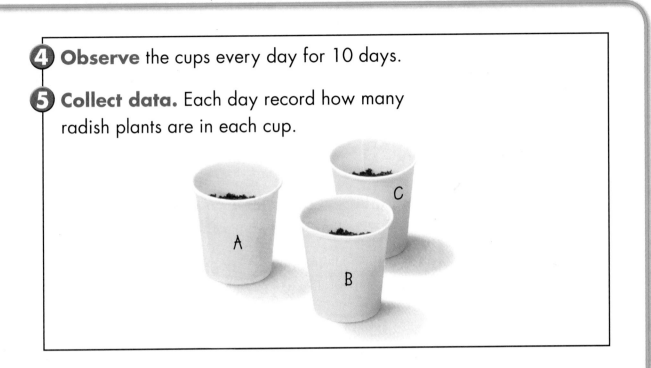

Effect of Salt on Radish Plants

Day	Number of Radish Plants		
	Cup A (tap water)	**Cup B** (salty water)	**Cup C** (very salty water)
Day 1			
Day 2			
Day 3			
Day 4			

Explain Your Results

1. Describe and compare what happened in each cup. Use the **data** you **collected.**

2. **Draw a Conclusion** How does salt affect radish plants?

Go Further

Are there plants that can survive in salty soils? Make a plan to answer this or other questions you may have.

Chapter 5 Reviewing Key Concepts

Focus on the BIG Idea Change allows some plants and animals to survive and reproduce. Change causes others to die or move to new locations.

Lesson 1

How do living things change their environment?
- Living things compete for food, water, light, shelter, or living space.
- As they survive, many living things change the environment. Some changes are helpful to living things and some may be harmful.

Lesson 2

How do changes in the environment affect living things?
- Not enough water, too much water, volcanic eruptions, and fires affect living things.
- Some living things survive when the environment changes. Others die or move to new locations.

Lesson 3

How do living things compare to those of long ago?
- Fossils show how changes in the environment caused many kinds of living things to disappear.
- Fossils show ways many extinct plants and animals were like plants and animals alive today. Fossils also show ways many extinct plants and animals were different from plants and animals alive today.

Cross-Curricular Links

English–Language Arts

Building Vocabulary

Look again at page 152. Observe the picture behind the words *competition* and *habitat*. Write a paragraph explaining how the picture illustrates the two words. How is competition, for instance, leading to a change in a habitat?

Mathematics

Extinct Plants and Animals

About 65 million years ago, many plants and animals became extinct. Some scientists believe that about $\frac{4}{5}$ of the kinds of living things alive then became extinct. What fraction of the kinds of living things survived?

History–Social Science

Changing Rivers

Like beavers, humans build dams that block rivers. Find out more about how dams change the environments where they are built. Present what you learn to your class.

Challenge!

English–Language Arts

Fossils

Fossils of many different kinds of plants and animals have been found. Use the library-media center to find pictures of fossils. Choose one fossil. Write a description of it. Was it a plant or animal? Tell what you think its life was like.

Chapter 5 Review/Test

Use Vocabulary

competition (page 157)	**fossil** (page 168)
extinct (page 168)	**habitat** (page 157)

Write the correct word in each blank. If you have trouble, read the listed page again.

1. A(n) _____ plant or animal no longer lives on Earth.

2. The place where a living thing makes its home is its _____.

3. _____ happens between living things that need the same resource.

4. The remains or mark left by a dead organism is a(n) _____.

Think About It

5. Suppose the number of rabbits in an area increases. Predict the change in the amount of grass.

6. Explain how beavers that build dams help other living things.

7. How did some animals survive the eruption of Mt. St. Helens?

8. Suppose fossils of plants adapted to a swamp are in a desert. What changed to allow this?

Process Skills

9. Infer A fossil skull has sharp, pointed teeth. What did the animal most likely eat?

10. Predict A gardener plants purple loosestrife near a stream. What will most likely happen nearby?

11. Interpret Data The bar graph shows grass and lemmings in a tundra. What may happen in Year Three?

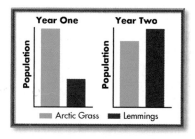

12. Make Inferences Make a graphic organizer, as shown. List facts about Mt. St. Helens' eruption. Infer changes after other times that the mountain erupted.

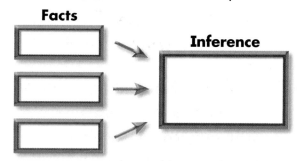

13. Writing in Science

Descriptive What changes take place after a severe forest fire?

California Standards Practice

Write the letter of the correct answer.

14. When fertilizer is put on crops, what may grow?

  A the number of farms

  B the algae in streams

  C the fish

  D the lakes and rivers

15. What could happen to animals competing for food?

  A They could eat anything alive.

  B They could stop eating.

  C They could move to a new location.

  D They could only drink water.

16. Which benefit from beavers building dams?

  A animals that need still water

  B trees cut for the dams

  C animals that need flowing water

  D plants covered by pond water

17. Which change caused by a forest fire is helpful?

  A destroying animal homes

  B adding ash to soil

  C burning animals' hiding places

  D putting smoke in the air

18. Why do some lakes dry up for good?

  A It turns cold and wet.

  B Animals leave the environment.

  C People take too much water.

  D The plants in the area change.

19. What is true about an extinct plant or animal?

  A It never leaves a mark.

  B It can resemble those alive today.

  C It was never adapted.

  D It failed to change the environment.

20. What is happening to the forest in the picture?

  A competition between trees

  B extinction of trees

  C destruction of forest habitat

  D trees becoming fossils

Moon Trees

Astronaut Stuart Roosa took seeds with him into space.

Did you know there might be Moon trees growing where you live? You may be asking yourself, "What do Moon trees look like? Did they come from the Moon? Where are they growing on Earth?"

Moon trees did not come from the Moon. They are trees grown from seeds that traveled to the Moon and back on the Apollo 14 mission in 1971.

Astronaut Stuart Roosa took the seeds into space. Astronaut Roosa worked for the U.S. Forest Service fighting forest fires before he joined NASA. He loved forests and wanted to protect them. He took seeds of pine, sycamore, redwood, Douglas fir, and sweet gum into space to honor the U.S. Forest Service.

A third-grade class in Indiana made this sign for their Moon tree. Astronaut Roosa's son, Col. Christopher Roosa, visited the tree with the students and their teacher.

MOON TREE

THIS SYCAMORE WAS GROWN FROM A
SEED THAT TRAVELED TO THE
MOON AND BACK ON
APOLLO XIV JANUARY 1971.
PRESENTED TO CAMP KOCH IN 1976
REDEDICATED APRIL 10, 2003

"LONG MAY OUR MOON TREE LIVE"

When the seeds were brought back to Earth, scientists examined them to see if space travel had changed them in any way. Then they were planted. No one knew what the trees would look like or even if they would grow.

The Moon trees grew until they were big enough to plant outside. People all over the world began to learn about the Moon trees. They wanted one of their own. In 1975 and 1976, the little trees were sent to places around the world. Most Moon trees were sent to schools, parks, and public buildings.

Today you can find a Moon tree growing near the Liberty Bell in Philadelphia. Another grows at the White House. Let NASA know if you find that a Moon tree is growing where you live.

You can see this Moon tree at the NASA Goddard Space Flight Center in Maryland.

Lab zone Take-Home Activity

What are ways space travel might have changed the Moon tree seeds? Write a paragraph listing the changes. Describe the effects the changes might have on the way they would grow.

Paul Sereno: Expert Dinosaur Hunter

Paul Sereno

When he was a boy, Paul Sereno liked to go on nature hikes with his brothers. He brought home insects to add to his collection. Paul went to college to study art. However, while he was in college, Paul decided he wanted to become a paleontologist—a scientist who studies ancient life.

Paleontologists like Dr. Sereno try to find fossils to piece together the story of what life was like long ago. Dr. Sereno and his team have found many kinds of dinosaurs that are new to science.

Dr. Sereno's team made a discovery in Africa. A giant claw lying in the desert was the first clue. Dr. Sereno and his team carefully dug for more bones. They found a huge skeleton of a dinosaur. Its skull was long with crocodile-like teeth. Dr. Sereno named the new dinosaur *Suchomimus,* which means "crocodile mimic."

It sometimes takes years for paleontologists to make sense of what they find. But their hard work often leads to new discoveries.

Lab zone Take-Home Activity

Find out about newly discovered dinosaurs. List them by name, type of dinosaur, and where found.

Unit B Summary

Chapter 4

What are ways living things survive in their environments?

- Adaptations help plants and animals meet their needs.
- Living things that live in oceans, deserts, tundra, forests, grasslands, and wetlands are different from one another because their environments are different.
- Some plants and animals are adapted to life in fresh water, salt water, or a mixture of fresh and salt water.

Chapter 5

How does change affect the survival of living things?

- Living things and natural events can change the environment. The changes may help or harm living things.
- When an environment changes, some plants and animals survive while others die or move to new locations.
- Fossils show us how extinct plants and animals are alike and different from plants and animals alive today. Fossils can also show how the environment has changed.

Lab zone Full Inquiry

Experiment How do some leaves stay dry in a rain forest?

Rain forests are very wet environments. Wet leaves can rot. However, a leaf's structure can help prevent this and help a plant survive. For example, leaves of certain shapes dry faster. In this experiment, you make models of leaves of different shapes. Then you test which shape drips faster. A shape that helps a leaf drip faster can help it dry faster.

Materials

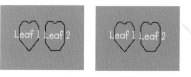

Leaf Shapes A

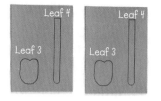

Leaf Shapes B

scissors

tub with water

8 paper clips

Process Skills

Every **experiment** must have a **hypothesis,** a testable statement.

Ask a question.

Some leaves are pointed at the end, while others are not pointed (Leaf Shapes A). Some leaves are long and narrow, while others are short and wide (Leaf Shapes B). Which leaf shape drips faster?

State a hypothesis.

Choose one variable to test. **Choice A:** Which drips faster—a leaf that is pointed or a leaf that is not pointed? **Choice B:** Which drips faster— a leaf that is long and narrow or a leaf that is short and wide? Write your **hypothesis.** Choice A is shown.

Identify and control variables.

In the model used in this experiment, the **variable** that you change is the shape of the leaf (pointed and not pointed, or narrow and wide). The variable you **observe** is how quickly each leaf drips. The area of the leaf is a variable you keep the same. All of the leaf shapes have the same area.

3LS3.a Students know that plants and animals have structures that serve different functions in growth, survival, and reproduction. **3IE5.a** Repeat observations to improve accuracy and know that the results of similar scientific investigations seldom turn out exactly the same because of differences in the things being investigated, methods being used, or uncertainty in the observation. **3IE5.e** Collect data in an investigation and analyze those data to develop a logical conclusion. (Also **3IE5.0**)

Test your hypothesis.

1 Cut out Leaf 1 and Leaf 2.

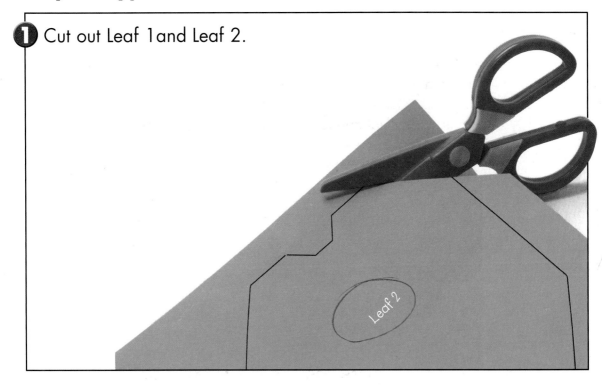

2 Dip Leaf 1 and Leaf 2 in water.

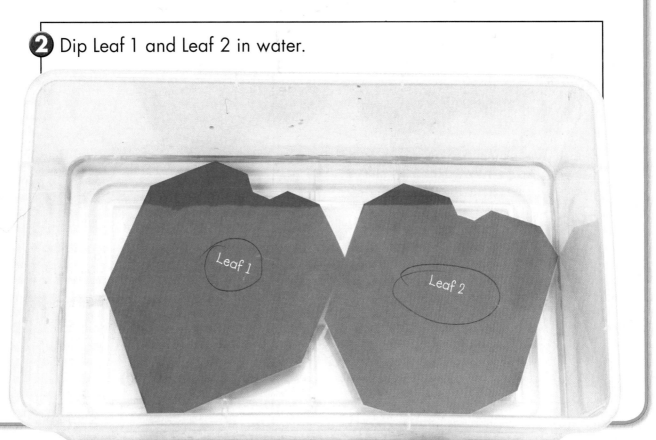

3 Use a paper clip to hang the leaves on a string.
Observe which leaf drips faster.

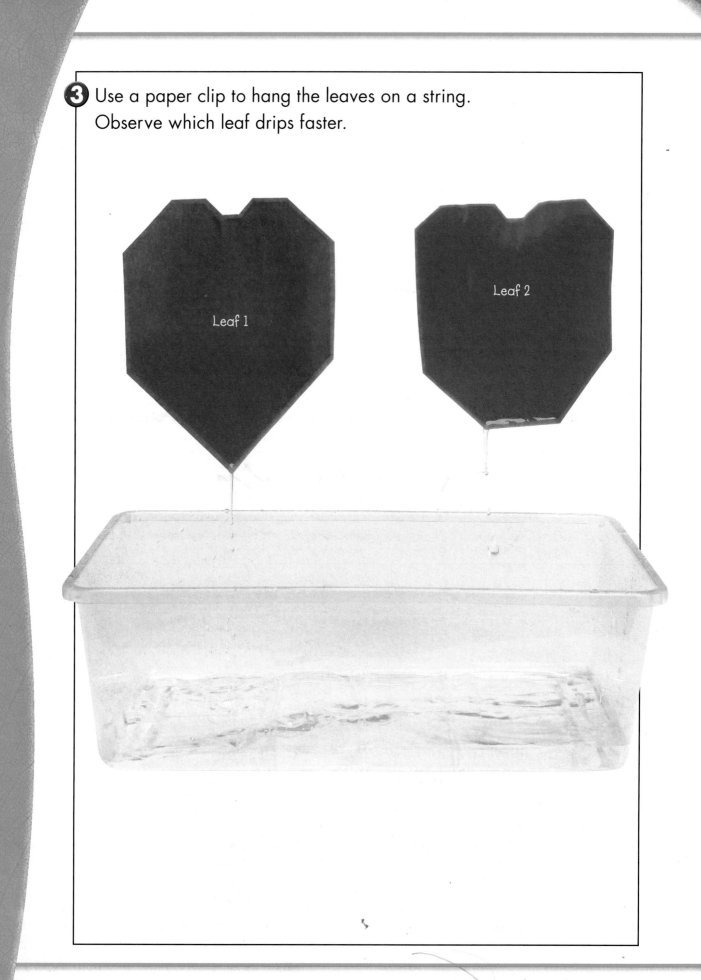

4 Repeat steps 1 through 3 to see if your observations are the same.

> Your results may not be exactly the same each time. Maybe you did not cut the leaves exactly the same way. Maybe you hung the leaves differently. Repeating an experiment and repeating your observations can help you get more accurate results.

Collect and record your data.

Choice A or B	Leaf Shapes	Observations	
		Trial 1	Trial 2
Choice A	Leaf 1		
	Leaf 2		
Choice B	Leaf 3		
	Leaf 4		

Interpret your data.

Compare which leaves drip faster. Compare your results with those of other student groups. Why might your results be different?

State your conclusion.

Tell which variable you tested. After analyzing your data, develop and **communicate** logical conclusions. Compare your hypothesis to your conclusions.

Go Further

Design and carry out a plan for an experiment using the leaf shapes you did not test. Analyze your data. State a logical conclusion.

Show What You Know

Model a Biome

Build or draw a model of the biome of your choice. Include plants and animals that live in that biome. Add labels that tell about the year-round weather pattern of the biome. Include labels in your model to show the adaptations of the plants and animals that live there.

Investigate Fossils

Obtain samples of several fossils or find pictures of fossils in the library-media center. Find out about the extinct plant or animals that left the fossils. Compare them with living plants or animals.

- If you have fossils, measure each with a metric ruler. Record your data. Write a short description of each fossil.

- Describe features of the fossils that show how extinct plants and animals were like living ones. Describe features that show how they were different from living ones.

- Infer what the environments were like when the extinct plants or animals were alive. Compare those environments with the environments of similar living plants and animals.

Write a Fantasy

Write a fantasy, which is a made-up story, about how an animal survives a flood. Include each of the following in your fantasy:

- a character that has a name
- a place where the story happened
- a beginning, middle, and ending to the story.

Read More About the Life Sciences

Look at other books about life sciences in your library. One book you may want to read is:

Nature's Paintbrush by Susan Stockdale

This book explores patterns and colors of plants and animals living together. The author uses bright, full-color drawings to show how patterns and color can help living things survive. Camouflage is only one way. Find out how flowers direct insects to nectar. See how birds attract partners, and frogs warn enemies to stay away.

Science Fair Projects

Using Scientific Methods
1. Ask a question.
2. State a hypothesis.
3. Identify and control variables.
4. Test your hypothesis.
5. Collect and record your data.
6. Interpret your data.
7. State your conclusion.
8. Go further.

Can temperature affect the growth of seeds?

Plants sprout from seeds.

Idea: Write a hypothesis and plan a test to see how temperature affects the growth of seeds. Place seeds in covered cups of wet soil in the refrigerator, at room temperature, and outside. Record how often and how fast they sprout and grow.

Does an animal's body covering help it survive cold temperatures?

Animals have body coverings that keep them warm.

Idea: Write a hypothesis and plan a test to see what kinds of materials best protect against cold. Wrap plastic jars of warm water with different materials. Record how fast the water cools.

How do dams change the environment?

Beavers and humans build dams.

Idea: Write a hypothesis and develop a model to test how dams affect the movement of water. Record the time that floating objects move from one end of a model stream to the other end. Dam the stream and repeat.

Write the letter of the correct answer.

1. Which of the following helps an animal blend into its surroundings?

  A camouflage

  B armor

  C poison

  D copying a more dangerous animal

2. Suppose that in a desert you find a fossil of a dinosaur that once lived in a swamp like the one pictured.

  Which of the following must be true?

  A Dinosaurs lived only in swamps.

  B Dinosaur fossils are found only in deserts.

  C When animals go extinct, the environment changes.

  D Swamps can change into deserts.

3. What adaptation helps kangaroo rats survive in a desert?

  A hunting during the day

  B drinking lots of water

  C getting water from food

  D storing water in a pouch inside their cheeks

4. What two animals might compete with one another for food?

  A coyotes and rabbits

  B coyotes and bobcats

  C bobcats and rabbits

  D bobcats and spotted owls

5. In which biome would you find many trees that lose their leaves each fall season?

  A tundra

  B desert

  C deciduous forest

  D coniferous forest

Unit B California Standards Practice

6. What does it mean for a type of plant or animal to be extinct?

  A The plant or animal is few in number.

  B The plant or animal no longer lives on Earth.

  C The plant or animal lives in many different places.

  D The plant or animal lives only in a few places.

7. What kind of teeth are adapted for eating plants?

  A flat teeth that grind food

  B pointed teeth that grasp food

  C sharp teeth that tear food

  D teeth with slits that filter food

8. What change might cause shrubs and grasses to replace trees?

  A more air

  B less space

  C less sunlight

  D less water

9. How does the covering on the animal shown below help the animal?

  A It keeps the animal cool.

  B It provides protection from other animals.

  C It helps the animal look like another kind of animal.

  D It helps the animal find and capture food.

10. Which of the following do beavers help when beavers improve their habitat?

  A plants and animals that need dry land

  B plants and animals that need an open stream

  C plants and animals that need still water

  D trees used for a dam

CALIFORNIA

11. Why are there few or no trees in the tundra?

  A The tundra is too wet.

  B The tundra is too steep.

  C The tundra is too hot.

  D The tundra is too cold.

12. A fish uses which structures to get oxygen from water?

  A scales

  B gills

  C eyes

  D fins

13. What do fossils show?

  A that all animals once ate only plants

  B that all plants in the past were like plants today

  C that there are many examples of extinct plants and animals

  D that only animals living today can fly

14. The picture below shows a volcanic eruption similar to the one that occurred at Mount St. Helens.

What is one effect that this eruption would have on the nearby environment?

  A Ash would cover the land.

  B Trees would live but shrubs and grasses would die.

  C Animals would not return.

  D The weather would become too cold for plants to grow again.

15. What structures help some cactus plants store water?

  A gills

  B leaves

  C fur

  D stems

CALIFORNIA

16. The picture below shows living things that might live in a cool rain forest.

Which living thing is best adapted to getting food from dead wood?

A A
B B
C C
D D

17. Why do trees grow very tall in a rain forest?

A to get more nutrients
B to get more air
C to get more sunlight
D to get more water

18. Which of the following lives in a salt marsh?

A crab
B buffalo
C cactus
D spotted owl

19. What do both people and beavers do that changes the habitat of other animals and plants?

A hunt for food
B plow land for farms
C cut down trees for wood
D start fires in forests

20. A fire can be helpful to which of the following?

A trees that survive the fire
B brush rabbits that hide in chaparral
C animals that make homes in dead wood
D whales that breathe with lungs

CALIFORNIA
Unit C

Earth Sciences

Palomar Observatory

San Diego, California

For 45 years, Mount Palomar in San Diego County was home to the world's largest telescope. The mirror in the Hale Telescope is 508 cm (over 16 feet) across! Scientists chose Mount Palomar because it is high above the ground in an area with many clear nights a year. In 1934, when construction began, it was also far away from city lights.

It took more than 20 years to build the observatory and the telescope. It was hard work to get it up the mountain! The mirror had to be specially ground and polished so it would be exactly the right size. Three tractors took 32 hours to push the mirror up the mountain. Engineers also had to build the dome that holds the telescope.

Though there are now larger telescopes, scientists still use the Hale Telescope on about 290 nights every year. Scientists use computers and other tools to help collect and interpret information with the telescope.

Find Out More

Research to find out more about telescopes in California.

Mount Palomar

- Mount Palomar is home to other telescopes and instruments. Find out more about these instruments and how they are used.

- Research the history of telescopes at Mount Palomar in California and in other places.

- If possible, visit an observatory near you. What kind of telescope does the observatory have? What can you see with it?

Chapter 6
Objects in Space

3ES4.0 Objects in the sky move in regular and predictable patterns. As a basis for understanding this concept:

3ES4.d Students know that Earth is one of several planets that orbit the Sun and that the Moon orbits Earth.

3ES4.c Students know telescopes magnify the appearance of some distant objects in the sky, including the Moon and the planets. The number of stars that can be seen through telescopes is dramatically greater than the number that can be seen by the unaided eye.

3IE5.0 Scientific progress is made by asking meaningful questions and conducting careful investigations. As a basis for understanding this concept and addressing the content in the other three strands, students should develop their own questions and perform investigations. (Also **3IE5.c**, **3IE5.d**)

Standards Focus Questions

- What moves around the Sun?
- How do we observe objects in space?

What can be observed in the nighttime sky?

star

solar system   planet   asteroid

DIGITAL

Chapter 6 Vocabulary

binoculars

telescope

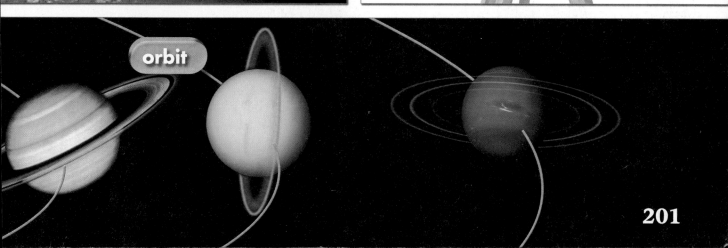

orbit

Explore How can you make a distance model of the solar system?

Materials

metric ruler
and meterstick

adding-machine tape

scissors

Process Skills

Using numerical
data can help you
measure, order,
and compare.

What to Do

1 **Measure** and cut adding-machine tape to the correct length for your planet. Roll up your tape.

Your teacher will help you select a planet.

Write your planet's name on the tape.

VENUS

56 cm

When all groups are ready, go into the hall. Your teacher will be the Sun.

2 A student in each group should stand by the Sun and hold the free end of the tape. Another student should walk down the hall, unrolling the tape.

Planet	Distance from the Sun in Model Length of Tape* (cm or m)
Mercury	30 cm or 0.30 m
Venus	56 cm or 0.56 m
Earth	77 cm or 0.77 m
Mars	120 cm or 1.2 m
Jupiter	400 cm or 4 m
Saturn	740 cm or 7.4 m
Uranus	1500 cm or 15 m
Neptune	2300 cm or 23 m

*Scale: 1 cm = about 1,940,000 km

Explain Your Results

Using your **observations** and **measurements,** compare the distances. **Infer** how the distance from the Sun might affect a planet's temperature.

3ES4.d Students know that Earth is one of several planets that orbit the Sun and that the Moon orbits Earth. **3IE5.c** Use numerical data in describing and comparing objects, events, and measurements.

Predict

Predict means to **infer** what might happen next.

Science Report

Sky Report

Andromeda is a spiral galaxy, a huge group of stars in the shape of a disk. Last night the Moon was not shining and I could see Andromeda with just my eyes. It appeared to be a dim star. When I used a pair of binoculars to view it, it appeared to be a fuzzy star.

Apply It!

Based on what you've read, predict what the sky reporter will see when he or she looks at Andromeda through a high-powered telescope. Make a graphic organizer to help you.

I Know   **I Predict**

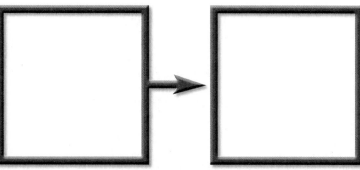

You Are There!

You look toward the sky on a clear day. How bright the Sun is! But don't look directly at it! You must turn your eyes away. Staring at the Sun can harm your eyes. Our world and many other objects travel around this huge, bright ball. What do you see when you look at these objects moving in space?

Standards Focus 3ES4.0 Objects in the sky move in regular and predictable patterns. As a basis for understanding this concept:
3ES4.d Students know that Earth is one of several planets that orbit the Sun and that the Moon orbits Earth.

What moves around the Sun?

Many objects move around the Sun. Other objects move around some of the planets, including around Earth.

The Sun

The Sun is a **star**, a huge ball of hot, glowing gases. How big is a star, such as the Sun? In a word—huge! The Sun is about 100 times as wide as Earth. How hot is a star, such as the Sun? In a word—hot! The temperature on the surface of the Sun is about 5,500°C. That's about 15 times as hot as boiling water. The Sun's center is much hotter.

The Sun looks larger and brighter than stars you see at night because it is the star closest to Earth. The other stars in the sky look small and fixed in place because they are so far away.

The Sun causes Earth and other objects to move around it in patterns. Since Earth is moving, figuring out these patterns was complicated. Getting accurate measurements took a long time.

Our star, the Sun, is close to Earth compared to other stars.

1. **✓Checkpoint** Why does the Sun appear brighter than other stars?

2. **✎ Writing in Science Descriptive**
   Describe what the Sun is like without the benefit of looking at it.

How Objects in the Solar System Move

We live on the planet Earth. A **planet** is a large, nearly round, ball-shaped object that travels in a path around the Sun. No other objects are near a planet's path. Many planets have moons. The Sun, the planets and their moons, and other objects that orbit the Sun make up the **solar system.** The Sun is the center of the solar system.

Objects that move around the Sun travel in regular patterns that can be predicted. The path an object takes as it moves around the Sun is its **orbit.** Each planet travels in an orbit that is slightly oval in shape. The strong pull of the Sun's gravity holds each planet in its orbit.

In this diagram sizes and distances are not true to scale.

Jupiter
Jupiter orbits the Sun in 12 years. The average temperature is 148°C below freezing.

Earth
Earth orbits the Sun in 365 days, or 1 year. The average surface temperature on your home planet is 15°C.

Mercury
Mercury orbits the Sun in 88 days. The average surface temperature is 167°C.

Venus
Venus orbits the Sun every 225 days. It has an average surface temperature of 462°C.

Asteroid Belt
Most asteroids orbit the Sun between Mars and Jupiter.

Mars
Mars orbits the Sun in 687 days. The average surface temperature is 55°C below freezing.

Planets of the Solar System

There are eight known planets in the solar system. The four planets nearest the Sun are Mercury, Venus, Earth, and Mars. These planets orbit the Sun in the fastest times. The planets farthest from the Sun are Jupiter, Saturn, Uranus, and Neptune. These planets take many Earth years to orbit the Sun just once.

Between the planets, thousands of rocky objects called asteroids orbit the Sun. An **asteroid** is a large piece of rock. Asteroids are found in various shapes and sizes.

1. ✓**Checkpoint** List the planets that orbit the Sun from closest to farthest away.

2. ✎ Writing in Science **Narrative** Suppose you are traveling in a spaceship. Write a story about passing by each of the known planets.

Pluto   *Charon, a moon of Pluto*

A Dwarf Planet

A small, cold, rocky object called Pluto orbits far from the Sun. It used to be called a planet. But Pluto is very small, smaller than Earth's moon. Pluto also has an odd orbit. In 2006, scientists decided to call Pluto a "dwarf planet." Dwarf planets are small, round objects that orbit the Sun. They are not moons.

Saturn
Saturn takes 29 years to orbit the Sun. The average temperature of Saturn is 178°C below freezing.

Uranus
Uranus takes 84 years to orbit the Sun. The average temperature of Uranus is 216°C below freezing.

Neptune
Neptune orbits the Sun once every 165 years. The average temperature of Neptune is 214°C below freezing.

keyword: **planet**
code: gr3p206

The Path of the Moon

While Earth orbits the Sun, the Moon orbits Earth. The Moon also turns slowly on its axis during this time. The Moon takes about 27 Earth days to complete one turn on its axis. At that time, the Moon has orbited Earth once. The Moon turns so slowly on its axis that the same side of the Moon always points toward Earth. We never see the other side from Earth. A spacecraft took the first pictures of the Moon's far side in 1959.

The Moon appears to rise in the sky. This effect is due to Earth's rotation.

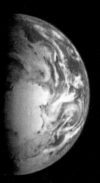

This photo taken from space shows that the Moon is small compared to Earth.

The Moon is the closest object to Earth. The Moon also is the brightest object in the night sky. It is so bright that you can see the Moon in the sky during the day. The Moon does not make its own light, however. The light you see from the Moon is light from the Sun that shines on the Moon and is reflected off it.

Notice the sunlight hitting half of Earth and half of the Moon in the picture. Sunlight always strikes half of Earth and half of the Moon. Viewed from Earth, however, the amount of the Moon that is lit changes a little each 24-hour period.

Besides the Moon, several star-like objects move across the fixed pattern of the stars. These are far-away planets that shine by light reflected from the Sun.

✓ Lesson Review

1. How do objects in the solar system move?

2. Describe how the Moon moves.

TARGET SKILL

3. **Predict** Suppose there was a planet closer to the Sun than Mercury. Would it take more or less time than Mercury to orbit the Sun?

How do we observe objects in space?

Telescopes are used to study planets, stars, and other objects in the sky.

Telescopes and the Night Sky

People are often startled the first time they look at details of the Moon through a telescope! A **telescope** is a tool for making distant objects appear nearer and larger. Many telescopes do this by magnifying light with pieces of glass called lenses. One problem is that most objects in the sky do not give off much light. Many telescopes have large, curved mirrors to collect more light. The reflected light is then directed to a lens. These telescopes give the brightest images of objects in the sky.

The Moon appears larger when viewed through a telescope. Can you see five dark, round spots? These are called seas, which are low, flat areas on the Moon's surface.

You might use a telescope like this one to observe the Moon, planets, and stars. Never use a telescope or any other instrument to study the Sun.

Moon

DIGITAL

Look for Active Art animations at www.pearsonsuccessnet.com

Standards Focus 3ES4.c Students know telescopes magnify the appearance of some distant objects in the sky, including the Moon and the planets. The number of stars that can be seen through telescopes is dramatically greater than the number that can be seen by the unaided eye.

You can see Saturn with just your eyes.

• Saturn

You can see the rings of Saturn with a telescope.

Binoculars are two telescopes joined together as a unit. You use both eyes to look through binoculars. Binoculars usually don't magnify objects as well as telescopes do. However, binoculars give sharp, clear images of many objects in the sky.

Before you study the sky outdoors, you should find out what is in the sky with up-to-date charts and pictures. Next, choose a time and a place to look up at the sky. Objects are best seen in dark skies on clear nights. Darker skies are found away from the lights of the city. Then, when you are outdoors, carefully observe the sky with your eyes. Finally, look through binoculars or a telescope that is held firmly in place.

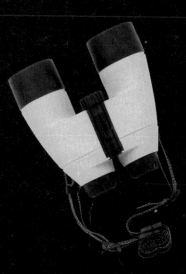

Binoculars help you see objects in the sky. Do not use them to view the Sun.

1. ✔ **Checkpoint** Why do people use telescopes to view the night sky?

2. **Predict** Suppose you observe Saturn. Will Saturn appear in the same place in the sky two weeks after first observing it? How will you be able to tell?

Viewing Distant Planets

You can see Mercury, Venus, Mars, Jupiter, and Saturn without a telescope. But if you use a telescope, you can see how it helps you to study these distant planets. A telescope can help you see that the surface of Mars is slightly red in color. A telescope can show colorful bands of clouds above the surface of Jupiter. You may also be able to see Jupiter's Great Red Spot, a storm three times the size of Earth.

The surface of Mercury is covered with craters. Steep slopes and long cliffs cut through the craters.

Thick clouds that surround Venus trap heat. More than 1,000 volcanoes are hidden behind these clouds.

Mars has bright white ice caps at its poles. You can see them clearly against the planet's red soil.

Jupiter is the largest planet in the solar system. Its Great Red Spot is actually a huge storm. Sometimes, you can see 4 of Jupiter's 63 known moons.

Some planets are too far away from Earth for people to see details, even with a large telescope. These planets include Uranus and Neptune. The United States has sent space probes to take pictures and make measurements of these planets.

1. ✓**Checkpoint** Which planets can be seen without the aid of a telescope? Which are too far away to see details, even with a large telescope?

2. ✏️ *Writing in Science* **Descriptive** Suppose you are given the chance to look at one of the planets through a high-powered telescope. Choose a planet and describe what you would see. Use resource materials from the library-media center.

Like other large planets, Uranus is surrounded by rings.

Neptune looks light blue and is surrounded by rings. Bands of clouds appear and disappear.

Viewing Stars and Galaxies

Think about being outside on a clear, dark night. You see thousands of tiny, twinkling stars. When you use a telescope, you see even more stars. They appear different in size, color, and brightness. What appears as a single point of light may be a *galaxy*. A galaxy is a group of stars, dust, and gas that are arranged together.

Different Kinds of Stars

The Sun is a very bright star because it is the star closest to Earth. It would thus be easy to think that bright stars in the nighttime sky are closer to Earth than dim ones. Other features affect the brightness of stars, however. Stars differ in size. Stars differ in the amount of light they make. There are small stars that make more light than big stars. Stars differ in color. There are red, yellow, and blue stars. Stars that appear dim may be closer to Earth than stars that appear bright.

Stars differ in size, color, amount of light they make, and distance from Earth. These features affect how stars appear in the sky.

New stars are forming in this huge cloud of gas and dust.

A galaxy is a huge group of stars, dust, and gas. The Sun and its planets are in the Milky Way Galaxy, which has more than 400 billion stars!

The Magellanic Cloud orbits our galaxy. It is made up of two galaxies. Each is smaller than our Milky Way.

Telescopes show that many galaxies appear to spin, which gives them a spiral shape.

✓ Lesson Review

1. Why can some planets be seen without the aid of a telescope while others cannot?

2. How do telescopes help scientists learn about stars and galaxies?

3. **Predict** Use a graphic organizer to predict the appearance of Saturn when viewed through a telescope.

Math in Science

Patterns in Planets

The distance of a planet from the Sun affects the time needed to orbit the Sun.

The first column in the chart below lists some of the planets in the order of their distances from the Sun, from the nearest to farthest. The second column gives the length of time each planet takes to complete one orbit.

Planet	Time of Orbit
Jupiter	12 Earth years
Saturn	29 Earth years
Uranus	84 Earth years
Neptune	165 Earth years

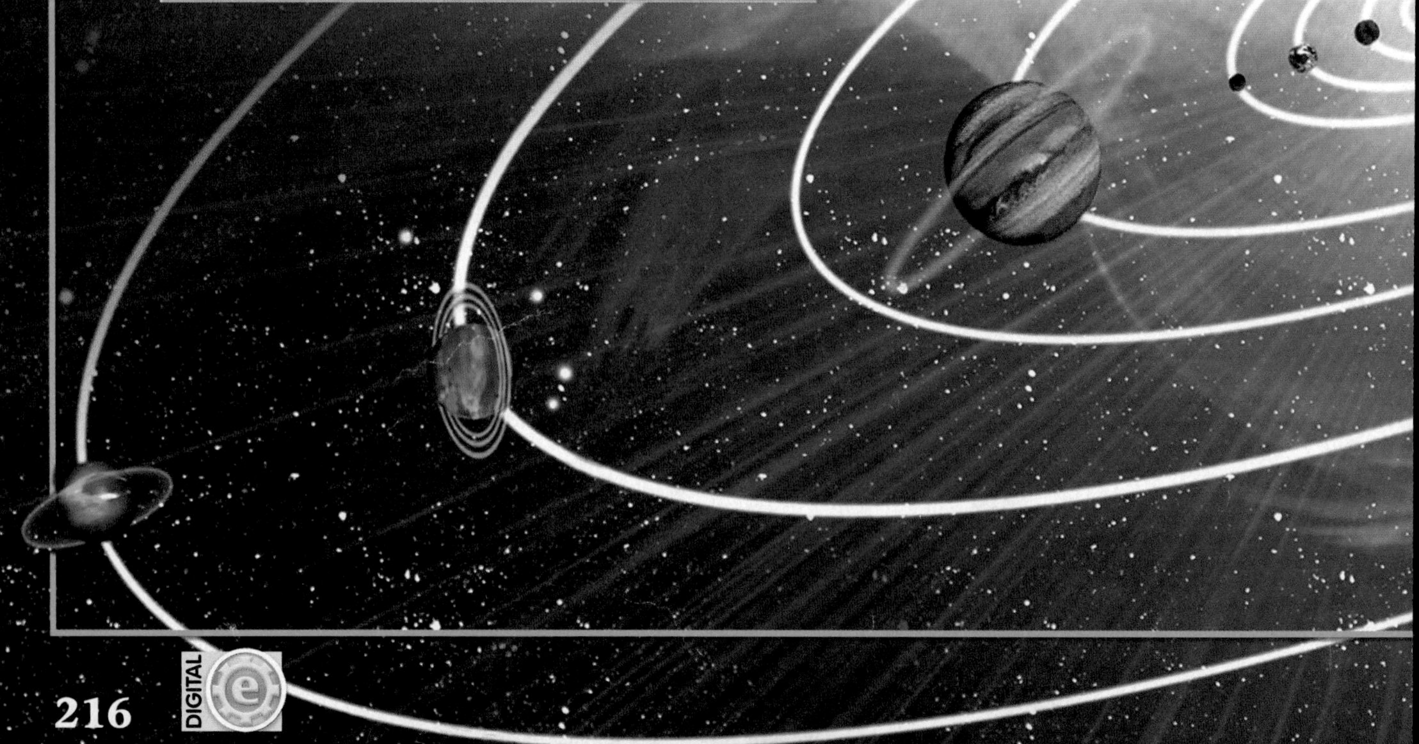

Use the chart to answer the questions.

 Which of the following planets takes the shortest time to orbit the Sun?

    A. Jupiter   B. Saturn   C. Neptune   D. Uranus

 How much longer is the orbit time of Neptune than that of Jupiter?

    A. 136 Earth years   B. 226 Earth years

    C. 260 Earth years   D. 153 Earth years

3 What pattern do you see in the distance of a planet from the Sun and the planet's orbit time?

    A. Planets closer to the Sun take longer to orbit the Sun.

    B. Planets farther from the Sun take longer to orbit the Sun.

    C. Planets farther from the Sun take a shorter time to orbit the Sun.

    D. The chart shows no pattern.

Lab zone Take-Home Activity

Choose two charts of information about things in newspapers and magazines. Write down what patterns you see in the charts.

Investigate How does a telescope change how objects look?

Materials

convex lens

magnifier

unsharpened pencil

What to Do

1 Hold the magnifier in front of your eye. **Observe** a pencil through the magnifier. Move the pencil forward until it is in focus.

2 Repeat step 1 using the lens.

Process Skills

You **predict** when you describe possible results of an **investigation**.

3ES4.c Students know telescopes magnify the appearance of some distant objects in the sky, including the Moon and the planets. The number of stars that can be seen through telescopes is dramatically greater than the number that can be seen by the unaided eye. **3IE5.d** Predict the outcome of a simple investigation and compare the result with the prediction.

3 Make a simple telescope. Hold the magnifier near your eye. Hold the lens in front of the magnifier so you can see through both of them.

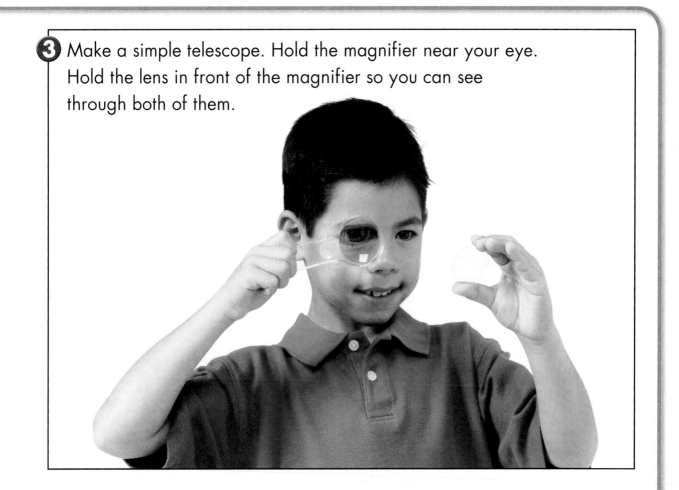

4 **Predict** how a distant object will look through the telescope. Record. Then move the lens back and forth until the object comes into focus.

Appearance of Distant Object Through Telescope

Prediction	Observation

Explain Your Results

1. Compare your **observation** with your **prediction.**

2. **Infer** How can a telescope help you study distant objects in the sky?

Go Further

What might happen if you switch the positions of the lens and magnifier? Find out.

Focus on the BIG Idea

The Moon, stars, and some of the known planets can be observed in the nighttime sky. Telescope or binoculars help by magnifying the appearance of objects in the sky.

Lesson 1

What moves around the Sun?

- Earth is one of several planets that orbits the Sun. Earth orbits the Sun in a path similar to that of the other planets.
- The Moon orbits Earth.
- Planets that reflect sunlight appear as star-like objects that move across the sky's star patterns.

Lesson 2

How do we observe objects in space?

- Telescopes and binoculars magnify the appearance of some distant objects in the sky.
- Mercury, Venus, Mars, Jupiter, and Saturn are planets that can be seen without the aid of a telescope. Uranus and Neptune are planets that can be seen only with the aid of a telescope.
- The number of stars seen through telescopes is much greater than the number seen with the unaided eye.

Cross-Curricular Links

English–Language Arts

Building Vocabulary

Look again at page 200. Identify the picture behind the terms *solar system*, *planet*, and *asteroid*. Write a paragraph explaining how the terms relate to the picture.

Mathematics

Math in Models

Suppose that you are making a model of the solar system. The model Earth is 2 cm wide. The Sun is about 100 times wider than Earth. About how wide should the model Sun be?

Visual and Performing Arts

Orbiting Art

Draw the eight known planets in their orbits around the Sun. Include the Moon's orbit around Earth. Be sure to label the planets.

Challenge!

English–Language Arts

Telling About Telescopes

Choose a famous telescope, such as the telescope at Mount Palomar. Use library-media center resources to learn more about the telescope and how scientists have used it. Make a booklet describing what you learn.

Chapter 6 Review/Test

Use Vocabulary

asteroid (page 207)	**planet** (page 206)
binoculars (page 211)	**solar system** (page 206)
orbit (page 206)	**star** (page 205)
	telescope (page 210)

Use the term from the list that completes each sentence. If you can't answer a question, read the listed page again.

1. A(n) _____ is a large piece of rock that orbits around the Sun.

2. The path a planet takes as it moves around the Sun is its _____.

3. Two telescopes joined together as a unit are (a) _____.

4. A(n) _____ is a large, round, ball-shaped object that orbits the Sun.

5. A giant ball of hot, glowing gases is a(n) _____.

6. A(n) _____ is a tool that magnifies objects that are far away.

7. The Sun, orbiting planets, moons, and other objects make up the _____.

Think About It

8. Why are telescopes important to people who study the night sky?

9. Compare the motions of Earth and the Moon.

10. Two stars are the same size and make the same amount of light. Why might one of them appear brighter?

11. **Process Skills** **Form Questions** What is one question that could be answered by observing Mars through a high-powered telescope?

12. **Predict** Would the orbit time for any planet farther from the Sun than Neptune be longer or shorter than Neptune's? Use a graphic organizer like the one below.

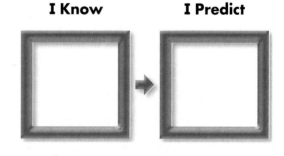

I Know	I Predict

13. **Writing in Science** **Descriptive** Write a paragraph describing the solar system and Earth's place in it.

California Standards Practice

Write the letter of the correct answer.

14. How should you look at the Sun?
- **A** with a telescope
- **B** with your eyes
- **C** with binoculars
- **D** You should never look directly at the Sun with your eyes, a telescope, or binoculars.

15. Compared to the unaided eye, how many stars can be seen through a telescope?
- **A** a greater number
- **B** a lesser number
- **C** the same number
- **D** none of the above

16. In the diagram of the planets closest to the Sun, which is Venus?

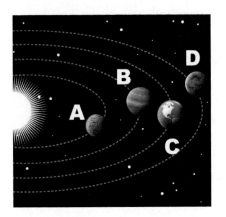

17. Which object orbits Earth?
- **A** the Sun
- **B** Venus
- **C** the Moon
- **D** the Asteroid

18. Which object can you see without a telescope?
- **A** Saturn
- **B** Uranus
- **C** Neptune
- **D** the Asteroid

19. Which of the following describes Earth?
- **A** farthest planet from the Sun
- **B** closest asteroid to the Sun
- **C** smallest star that orbits the Sun
- **D** one of several planets that orbit the Sun

20. How do telescopes make objects appear larger and clearer?
- **A** shining more light onto objects
- **B** bringing objects closer
- **C** magnifying the appearance of objects
- **D** taking large pictures of small objects

The Hubble Space Telescope

You can use a telescope to make stars and other objects in space easier to see. Imagine how many stars you could see with a telescope 13.2 meters (43.5 feet) long and 4.2 meters (14 feet) wide. Imagine it weighing 11,000 kilograms (24,000 pounds)—about the size of a school bus. You would not be taking it over to a friend's house to look at stars. A telescope this size would not fit in a car, but it did fit in a space shuttle.

In 1990, NASA launched the Hubble Space Telescope. The Hubble stays in space about 600 kilometers (375 miles) above Earth. It orbits Earth every 97 minutes.

The Hubble collects information from space and sends it to scientists on Earth every day. It provides detailed images of Mars and Pluto. It helps scientists understand more about Uranus and Neptune. The Hubble also has helped scientists learn about objects outside our solar system. It provides information about black holes, quasars, and the birth and death of stars.

An astronaut works on the Hubble Space Telescope.

Take-Home Activity

If you have Internet access at home or at the library, go to the NASA Web site located at http://hubblesite.org and look at images from the Hubble.

The solar panels provide power to the telescope.

225

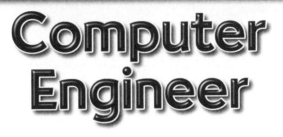

Computer Engineer

Do you like reading adventure stories about going to distant planets? Most planets are too far away for live astronauts to explore them. NASA sends certain spacecraft without people instead. They carry robots that can explore planets the same way astronauts can. Computer engineers help design the robots.

People such as Dr. Ayanna Howard study ways to use robots called rovers. These machines explore the surfaces of other planets. The rovers use computers to help find answers to problems.

Dr. Howard also tries to interest students in careers in math, science, and engineering. She speaks to students around the world about robots, computers, and technology.

People study in college to become computer engineers. Classes include math, engineering, and computer science.

Dr. Ayanna Howard

Mars
Exploration
Rover

Lab zone Take-Home Activity

Use objects from your home to make a model of a rover or other robot. Describe the parts of your robot and tell what your robot does. Compare your robot with the ones that explore other planets.

Chapter 7
Patterns in the Sky

How do objects in the sky move in patterns?

axis

rotation

revolution

DIGITAL

Chapter 7 Vocabulary

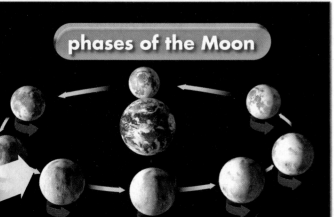

phases of the Moon

constellation

Explore How does the Sun's position affect a sundial's shadow?

Materials

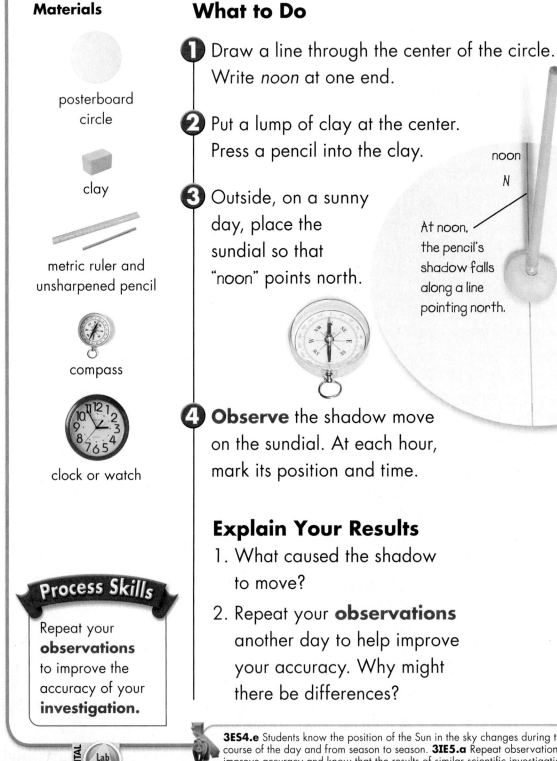

posterboard circle

clay

metric ruler and unsharpened pencil

compass

clock or watch

What to Do

1 Draw a line through the center of the circle. Write *noon* at one end.

2 Put a lump of clay at the center. Press a pencil into the clay.

3 Outside, on a sunny day, place the sundial so that "noon" points north.

noon

N

At noon, the pencil's shadow falls along a line pointing north.

4 **Observe** the shadow move on the sundial. At each hour, mark its position and time.

Explain Your Results

1. What caused the shadow to move?

2. Repeat your **observations** another day to help improve your accuracy. Why might there be differences?

3ES4.e Students know the position of the Sun in the sky changes during the course of the day and from season to season. **3IE5.a** Repeat observations to improve accuracy and know that the results of similar scientific investigations seldom turn out exactly the same because of differences in the things being investigated, methods being used, or uncertainty in the observation.

How to Read Science

Follow Instructions

- **Instructions** describe steps to **follow** to complete a task.
- Sometimes instructions have numbered steps. At other times, the steps do not have numbers. It is important to **observe** instructions carefully, following them in order.
- Read all of the instructions before you start. Make sure that you understand all of the instructions. Look for specific details that tell you how much or how many.

Lab Report

Instructions

Tracking a Shadow

What to Do

Cut a 3-inch circle from construction paper. Tape the paper circle onto a sunny window. Draw the outline of the circle's shadow on a large sheet of white paper near the window. Repeat this last step every 15 minutes for 2 hours.

Apply It!

Make a graphic organizer like the one shown. Fill it in to show the steps to follow when tracking a shadow. Then underline the words that tell how much, how big, or how often.

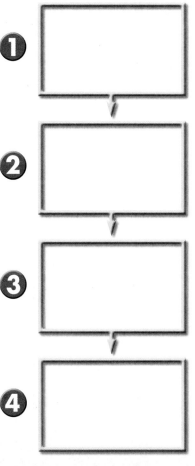

You Are There!

It's morning in California. Sunlight shines through your window. You remember seeing the Sun go down last night. Now it's coming up again on the other side of the sky. The Sun appears to rise higher and higher. You watch shadows slowly move a little across the wall. Then you climb out of bed to start your day. What causes this pattern of change?

DIGITAL

What are some patterns that repeat every day?

The Sun appears to move across the sky as Earth moves. Shadows get shorter toward noon and longer toward sunset. A regular pattern of day and night happens as Earth turns.

The Spinning Earth

You don't feel it, but Earth is moving. One way that Earth moves is by spinning around an imaginary line. One end of the line would stick out of Earth at the North Pole. The other end of the line would stick out of Earth at the South Pole. This imaginary line around which Earth spins is its **axis.**

Find Earth's axis in the drawing. If you could look down at the North Pole, you would see the Earth spinning in a counterclockwise direction. This direction is the opposite of the way the hands of a clock move. You could also say that Earth turns from west to east.

1. ✓**Checkpoint** Describe Earth's movement on its axis.

2. ✏**Writing in Science Descriptive** Suppose that you are in a spaceship near Earth's North Pole. Describe what you see as Earth turns on its axis.

The Sun appears to rise in the east.

The Sun appears to move across the sky, as Earth continues to rotate.

The Sun appears to set in the west.

Day and Night

Earth makes one complete spin, or **rotation,** on its axis every 24 hours. During this time, half of Earth always faces the Sun. That half of Earth has day. The half of Earth not facing the Sun has night. As Earth rotates, a different part of Earth faces the Sun.

Earth rotates at the same speed every day of the year. If you add the hours of sunlight and darkness together during one day and night, you will find that they always equal 24 hours, or one day. From Earth, it looks as though the Sun moves from east to west across the sky. But it's really Earth that moves.

Daytime begins when the Sun first appears over the horizon. As Earth rotates, this part of Earth is just beginning to face the Sun.

Shadow Patterns

Shadows form when sunlight strikes objects. The length and direction of shadows change during the day. You can observe the Sun's position using the shadow cast from an object, such as a tree.

The early morning Sun appears on the horizon in the east. Shadows stretch away from the Sun toward the west. Shadows are very long.

The Sun appears to move higher in the sky as Earth rotates on its axis. Shadows become shorter. Shadows are shortest around midday.

After midday, shadows stretch away from the Sun toward the east. The Sun appears to move lower in the sky toward the west. Shadows become longer. Shadows are again very long near sunset.

The length and direction of the shadow cast by this tree change during the day.

West East

Morning

West East

Midday

West East

Afternoon

✓ Lesson Review

1. Why does the Sun appear to move across the sky?

2. Describe the Sun's daily pattern using the shadow cast from a tree.

3. **Follow Instructions** Write steps for using a flagpole to show how a shadow changes from sunrise to sunset. Use a graphic organizer.

235

What patterns repeat every year?

Earth's tilt and movement around the Sun cause the seasons. The amount of light that Earth receives during different seasons causes seasonal patterns.

Earth's Tilt

You know that Earth rotates on its axis. Earth also moves around the Sun. A **revolution** is one complete trip an object makes around another object in the sky. Earth makes one revolution around the Sun in a year's time. Find Earth's axis in each part of the diagram. Earth's axis is not straight up and down. It is tilted. As Earth revolves around the Sun, Earth's axis always tilts in the same direction.

June

The northern half of Earth tilts toward the Sun. The northern half gets more direct sunlight and warmer temperatures than the southern half. It is summer in the northern half and winter in the southern half of Earth.

March

The northern and southern halves of Earth get about the same amounts of sunlight. Neither pole tilts toward the Sun or away from it. The northern half is getting warmer, but the southern half is getting cooler.

Standards Focus 3ES4.e Students know the position of the Sun in the sky changes during the course of the day and from season to season.

In some places on Earth's path around the Sun, the northern half of Earth is tilted toward the Sun. In other places along Earth's path, the southern half of Earth is tilted toward the Sun. The part of Earth that is tilted toward the Sun receives the most direct sunlight and is heated most. The part of Earth that is tilted away from the Sun receives the least direct sunlight and is heated least.

Direct sunlight covers less area. It is more concentrated. It heats Earth more than light that strikes at an angle.

December
The northern half of Earth tilts away from the Sun. This tilt causes the northern half of Earth to receive less sunlight and have colder temperatures than the southern half. It is winter in the north, but summer in the south.

Seasons

The changing amounts of sunlight and changing temperatures happen in patterns called *seasons*. Temperatures in the northern half of Earth, where you live, are usually warmest during the summer and coolest during the winter.

Look again at Earth's position in December on page 237. When the northern half of Earth tilts away from the Sun, this half of Earth gets less sunlight. The number of hours of darkness is greater than the number of hours of daylight in each 24-hour period. As spring approaches, daylight hours increase in number.

In the spring and fall, Earth's axis does not tilt toward the Sun or away from the Sun. The number of hours of daylight is about the same as the number of hours of darkness in each 24-hour period.

As winter approaches, the number of daylight hours becomes less. The chart on the next page shows the number of hours of daylight in the northern part of the United States.

The Sun's Position in the Sky

Another effect of Earth's tilted axis is that the Sun appears at different places in the sky in different seasons. During winter in the northern half of earth, the Sun appears lower and farther south in the sky. During summer the Sun appears more directly overhead and farther north.

June

When the Sun appears higher in the sky, there are more hours of daylight.

East

West

The way the Sun appears to cross the sky changes with the seasons.

Hours of Daylight in Northern United States

Month	Number of Hours of Daylight
December	9
March	12
June	15
September	12

December

The picture and the chart show the effects of Earth's tilted axis on the Sun's position and hours of daylight.

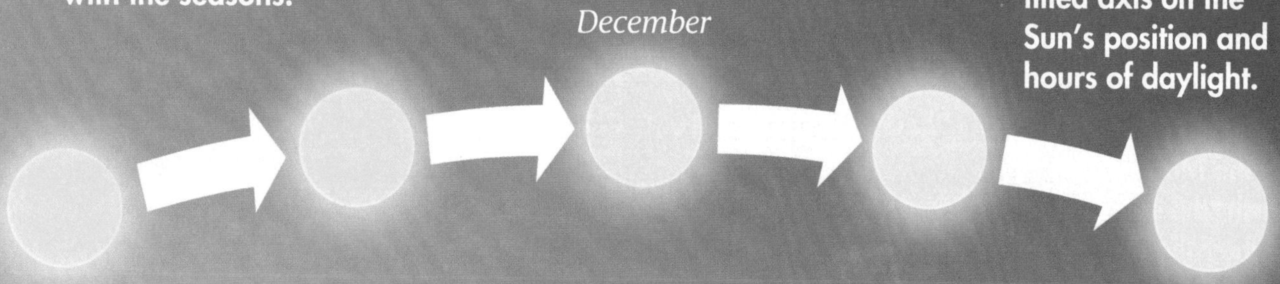

✓ Lesson Review

1. How does Earth's position and movement cause seasons?

2. Explain why the northern and southern halves of Earth get about the same amount of sunlight in spring and fall.

3. ✏ **Writing in Science Descriptive** Write a paragraph that describes your favorite season. Describe the position of the Earth in its orbit during that season.

What are Moon and star patterns?

The Moon's appearance follows a pattern of change over about four weeks. Patterns of stars seem to move across the sky during the night. Different groups of stars appear in different seasons.

The Moon and the Sun

Sometimes the Moon looks like a bright disk. At other times, the Moon looks like a half circle. Sometimes, it seems to be only a thin slice. For a short time each month, you can't see the Moon at all! Sunlight and the motions of the Moon and Earth cause these changes.

During a lunar eclipse, the Moon moves into and then out of Earth's shadow. A lunar eclipse is the only time when no side of the Moon is in sunlight.

As the Moon orbits Earth, the same side of the Moon always faces Earth.

Standards Focus 3ES4.a Students know the patterns of stars stay the same, although they appear to move across the sky nightly, and different stars can be seen in different seasons.
3ES4.b Students know the way in which the Moon's appearance changes during the four-week lunar cycle.

The moon appears as a *crescent* when less than half is lit.

First Quarter Phase
About a week after the New Moon, the Moon looks like a half circle.

As you can see on page 240, the Moon rotates on its axis and revolves around Earth. One half of the Moon is always in sunlight, except during a *lunar eclipse.* As the Moon moves around Earth, we see different amounts of the lit half. The changes in the way the Moon looks are called the **phases of the Moon.** The phases of the Moon repeat in a regular pattern about every four weeks.

The pictures show the Moon's phases. Starting as a *crescent,* more and more of the Moon appears each night until you see a complete circle of light, called a Full Moon. The Moon is *waxing* during this period. Then you see less and less of the Moon until you cannot see it at all during the New Moon. The Moon is *waning* during this period.

The Moon is *waxing* when more of the lit half of the Moon appears each night.

Full Moon Phase
About two weeks after the New Moon, you see all of the lit half of the Moon. It looks like a circle.

The Moon is *waning* when less of the lit half of the Moon appears each night.

1. ✓**Checkpoint** Describe the phases of the Moon.

2. **Follow Directions** Draw four circles on paper. Fill each in with one of the four Moon phases shown on this page. Cut them out. Write instructions for how to arrange them in the correct order in which they occur.

Third Quarter Phase
Three-fourths of the Moon's cycle is complete.

New Moon Phase
None of the Moon appears lit.

Crescent

The Little Dipper and the Big Dipper appear fixed in place in the early evening summer sky.

North Star

Star Patterns

Look up on a clear, dark night and you see thousands of twinkling stars. Many of the brighter ones seem to be in groups that make patterns or shapes. A group of stars that makes a pattern is a **constellation.** The stars in constellations appear not to move toward or away from each other. This is because they are far outside the solar system.

The diagrams on these pages show the Big Dipper and the Little Dipper. They look like cups with handles. These patterns are parts of the constellations Ursa Major (the Big Bear) and Ursa Minor (the Little Bear).

If you look at each of these star patterns in the early evening and again a few hours later, you will find that they have moved. The stars only appear to move. They seem to move across the sky because Earth is rotating on its axis.

North Star

Three hours later the positions of the Dippers have shifted. The pattern is one of a slow moving circle around a central star called the North Star.

 Look for Active Art animations at www.pearsonsuccessnet.com

242

North Star

Six hours later the Big and Little Dippers have revolved one-quarter of the way around the North Star. In twenty-four hours they will have completed a circle.

Look again at the diagrams of the Big and Little Dippers. The star at the end of the "handle" of the Little Dipper is the North Star. This star is directly over Earth's North Pole. Stars in the sky above the northern half of Earth appear to revolve around the North star.

1. ✓Checkpoint Why does the position of the Big Dipper change during the night?

2. ✎ Writing in Science **Narrative** Write a story about how the Big and Little Bears became constellations. Share your story with your class.

A photograph taken over a period of time shows how the positions of the stars change throughout the night. They make streaks of light called star tracks. The North Star is at the center of this picture.

Star Positions in Different Seasons

On a clear summer night you can see groups of stars such as the one that forms a W. This star pattern is the constellation Cassiopeia. However, on a winter night, you look for Cassiopeia and it's not where it was in summer. What has happened?

You know that Earth's tilt as Earth revolves around the Sun causes seasons. It also causes changes in the way stars appear to us. In summer, you see the nighttime sky from one point of view. Over the next six months, Earth moves in its orbit to the other side of the Sun. During this time, you face slightly different parts of space at night. By winter, you see the nighttime sky from a point of view that is different from summer.

North Star

During the summer in the Northern Hemisphere, Cassiopeia is low in the sky.

Different Stars in Different Seasons

Some stars, like those in Cassiopeia, are visible year-round, but their position changes. Other stars can be seen at only one time of year. During other times, these constellations are present in the sky during the daytime. If they were bright enough to outshine the Sun, you could see them all year!

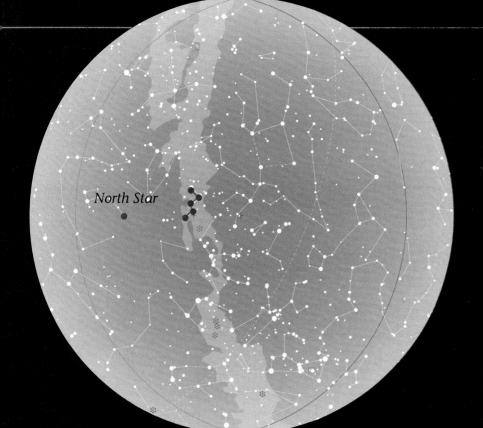

North Star

During late fall and winter in the Northern Hemisphere, Cassiopeia is almost directly overhead.

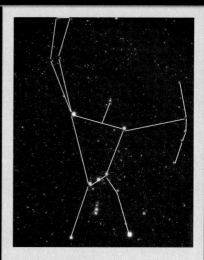

Orion

From late fall to early spring in the Northern Hemisphere, you can see the constellation Orion, the Hunter. The 3 stars close together make up Orion's belt. Nearby are 4 other bright stars. You can form Orion's outline with the 7 stars. Orion's position changes over several months. In March, its stars are too low in the sky to be seen.

A Winter Sky Star Pattern

High overhead on clear winter nights is a line of three bright stars close together. These stars are part of the constellation Orion, the Hunter. Ancient people thought that the three stars looked like the hunter's belt. In the summer, Orion is not visible at night.

✓ Lesson Review

1. Why does the Moon appear to change shape?

2. How does Earth's revolution affect your view of constellations?

TARGET SKILL

3. **Follow Instructions** Use a graphic organizer to show when and how to find the constellation Orion.

Comparing Times of Sunrises and Sunsets

As Earth revolves around the Sun, the amount of sunlight hitting different parts of Earth changes each day. The Sun looks like it rises above the horizon and sets below the horizon at different times. In the northern half of Earth, the Sun rises a little earlier and sets a little later each day from late December to late June. The days slowly have more daylight hours and fewer hours of darkness. The pattern is reversed in the southern half of Earth.

The chart below shows the pattern in the times of sunrise and sunset for four days during the year.

Sunrise and Sunset Standard Times for a City in the Northern Half of Earth		
Date	**Sunrise**	**Sunset**
March 21	5:52 A.M.	6:05 P.M.
June 21	5:16 A.M.	8:29 P.M.
September 21	6:38 A.M.	6:49 P.M.
December 21	7:15 A.M.	4:23 P.M.

Comparing Times

Use the chart to answer the following questions.

1 How many hours and minutes of daylight are there on March 21?

2 Which day has the most hours of daylight?

3 Which day has the fewest hours of daylight?

4 During which month would the southern half of Earth have its longest day? Explain.

Lab zone Take-Home Activity

Find the times of sunrise and sunset in your area daily for the next week. Compare the times and decide if the days are getting longer or shorter.

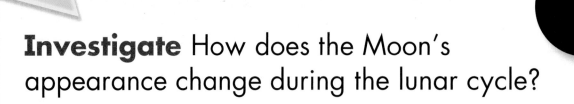

Investigate How does the Moon's appearance change during the lunar cycle?

You will build a model that shows the Moon's appearance during the phases of the lunar cycle.

Materials

shoe box with holes (prepared by teacher)

scissors and tape

flashlight and metric ruler

table tennis ball, black thread, thumbtack

Process Skills

You can use careful **observations** to help make good **predictions**.

What to Do

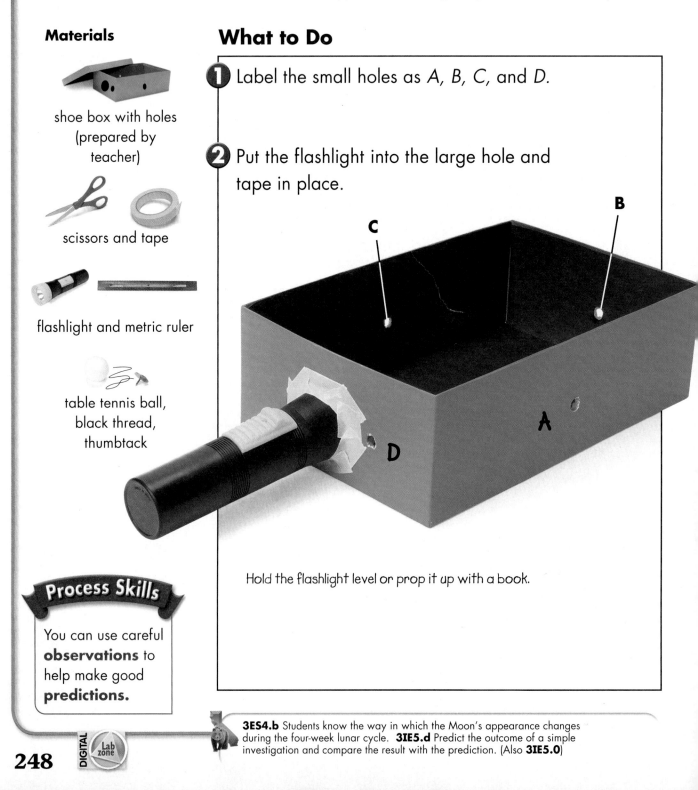

1 Label the small holes as *A*, *B*, *C*, and *D*.

2 Put the flashlight into the large hole and tape in place.

Hold the flashlight level or prop it up with a book.

3ES4.b Students know the way in which the Moon's appearance changes during the four-week lunar cycle. **3IE5.d** Predict the outcome of a simple investigation and compare the result with the prediction. (Also **3IE5.0**)

3 Attach the thread to the ball with a thumbtack.

about 4 cm

Tape the thread in place so the ball hangs down about 4 cm.

4 Look through holes A and B. Record your **observations.**

B

C

5 Predict how your model "moon" will appear through holes C and D. Record.

6 Look. Record. Compare with your **predictions.**

A

D

Phases of the Moon				
Hole	Drawing of Moon Phase		Name of Moon Phase	
A	◑		quarter moon	
B				
	Prediction	Observation	Prediction	Observation
C				
D				

Explain Your Results

1. You observed that the flashlight always lights half the "Moon." Why does the "Moon" appear to be completely full when viewed through one hole?

2. **Predict** What would you observe if you made a hole between holes A and B?

Go Further

How could you change your model to show more phases of the Moon? Develop a plan to answer this or any other question you may have.

Chapter 7 Reviewing Key Concepts

Focus on the BIG Idea

Earth spins on its axis as it travels around the Sun. The Moon revolves around Earth as Earth revolves around the Sun. These movements cause patterns in the appearance of objects in the sky.

Lesson 1

What are some patterns that repeat every day?
- Earth makes one complete rotation on its axis every 24 hours.
- As Earth rotates, the Sun appears to rise in the east, move across the sky, and set in the west.

Lesson 2

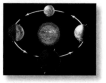

What patterns repeat every year?
- Earth's revolution around the Sun and the tilt of Earth's axis cause the seasons.
- Due to the tilt of the Earth's axis, the Sun appears to cross the sky in different places during the year.

Lesson 3

What are Moon and star patterns?
- As the Moon revolves around Earth, we see different amounts of sunlight reflected from the Moon. This causes the phases of the Moon, a pattern that repeats about every four weeks.
- Earth's rotation on its axis causes the stars to appear to move across the sky.
- As Earth revolves around the Sun, groups of stars are seen in different parts of the sky. Different stars can be seen in different seasons.

Cross-Curricular Links

English–Language Arts

Building Vocabulary

Look back at page 228. Identify the pictures behind the terms *axis, rotation,* and *revolution.* Tell how each word relates to the pictures.

Mathematics

Moon Phases

Look at the pictures on page 241. Use fractions to describe how much of the Moon's surface is lit during the following phases: First Quarter Moon, Full Moon, Third Quarter Moon, New Moon.

Visual and Perfoming Arts

Seasons on Stage

With a small group, act out the motions that show Earth moving around the Sun.

Challenge!

English–Language Arts

Moon Walk

In July 1969, Neil Armstrong became the first person to touch the Moon's surface. What did he find there? Use the library-media center to find out. Then write a paragraph explaining what Armstrong and later astronauts observed as they walked on the Moon's surface.

Chapter 7 Review/Test

Use Vocabulary

axis page 233	**revolution** page 236
constellation page 242	**rotation** page 234
phases of the Moon page 241	

Fill in the blanks with the correct vocabulary terms. If you have trouble answering a question, read the page listed in the box again.

1. Earth makes one complete spin, or _____, every 24 hours.

2. The _____ are caused by changes in the amount of the lit side of the Moon that can be seen from Earth.

3. A(n) _____ is a group of stars that make a pattern or shape in the sky.

4. Earth makes one _____ when it completes one trip around the Sun.

5. The imaginary line around which Earth spins is its _____.

Think About It

6. What would seasons be like if Earth's axis did not tilt?

7. During which season would a town in California have the fewest hours of daylight? Explain.

8. Why does a constellation appear to move in the nighttime sky?

9. **Process Skills** **Predict** The Full Moon is visible in the night sky. How long will it be before you see the Full Moon again?

10. **Infer** The shadow made by a tree is stretching to the east. What part of the day is it? Explain.

11. **TARGET SKILL** **Follow Instructions** Read the passage below. Then complete the graphic organizer to show how to find the North Star in the nighttime sky.
Find the Big Dipper. Look for two stars on the "cup" edge farthest from the handle. Think of a line between the two stars. Continue the line until it reaches the North Star.

1. _____
↓
2. _____
↓
3. _____
↓
4. _____

12. **Writing in Science**
Descriptive Write a paragraph describing how the daytime and nighttime skies change from summer to winter.

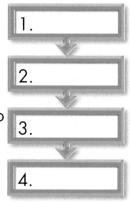

California Standards Practice

Write the letter of the correct answer.

13. Why do we see different stars in different seasons?

   A There are fewer clouds.

   B Stars revolve around Earth.

   C Earth revolves around the Sun.

   D Earth rotates on its axis.

14. Stars in constellations

   A appear to move across the sky.

   B appear to move apart.

   C are equally bright.

   D can be seen at noon.

15. A New Moon appears

   A about once a day.

   B about once a month.

   C about once a season.

   D about once a year.

16. The lit part of a Full Moon

   A faces Earth.

   B appears as a thin slice.

   C is three-fourths full.

   D cannot be seen.

17. The North Pole in winter

   A tilts away from the Sun.

   B tilts toward the Sun.

   C receives direct sunlight.

   D is straight up and down.

18. During which seasons will daytime and nighttime be about equal?

   A summer and winter

   B fall and summer

   C spring and summer

   D spring and fall

19. How much of a First Quarter Moon appears to be lit?

   A one quarter

   B one half

   C more than half

   D none

20. What causes the position of the Sun's path to shift, as shown in the drawing?

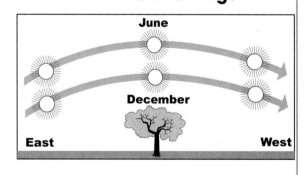

   A the pull of Earth's gravity

   B the tilt of Earth on its axis

   C the speed of Earth's rotation

   D how far away the Sun is

Galileo
1564–1642

Galileo was born in Italy in 1564. He studied medicine and mathematics at a university in Italy. He later became the head of the math department at another university.

Galileo became known for inventing science tools and experimenting. When he heard that someone had invented a tool that could magnify objects, he went to work to improve the telescope. Galileo soon had a telescope that could magnify objects twenty times.

Galileo used his telescope to make many discoveries. Galileo saw four moons revolving around Jupiter and different phases of Venus.

Does Earth revolve around the Sun? Galileo asked this meaningful question. Scientific progress often begins this way.

Galileo observed with his telescope. He knew that scientists do not rely on claims unless they are backed by observations. Galileo showed that Earth does revolve around the Sun.

Lab zone Take-Home Activity

Look up the work of Galileo. Describe other observations he made. Tell what his experiments led him to say about patterns in the sky.

Unit C Summary

Chapter 6

What can be observed moving in the nighttime sky?

- The solar system includes the Sun, the known planets and their moons, and other objects that orbit the Sun.
- We can see the Moon as it orbits Earth, while Earth orbits the Sun.
- Telescopes and binoculars help us to observe distant objects in the nighttime sky, such as the Moon and planets. These tools make objects appear larger and clearer.

Chapter 7

How do objects in the sky move in patterns?

- Earth rotates once every 24 hours and revolves once every year.
- Earth's movements cause the Sun to appear in a regular pattern during the day and from season to season.
- The Moon's appearance changes in a regular pattern called the phases of the Moon.
- Patterns of stars appear to move because of Earth's rotation and revolution. Some star patterns are visible only at certain times of the year.

Experiment How can you use a model to learn about patterns of stars in the sky?

The stars in the Big Dipper form a pattern. From our part of the universe, the pattern stays the same. Would it look the same from another part of the universe?

Materials

Drawing of the Big Dipper and Pattern for the Big Dipper Model

7 straws and 7 pieces of foil

metric ruler

scissors, tape, and clay

Process Skills

Some **models** can help you test a **hypothesis.**

Ask a question.

How would the Big Dipper appear if observed from another part of the universe?

State a hypothesis.

If the Big Dipper is observed from another part of the universe, will its appearance change a little, a lot, or not at all? Write your **hypothesis.** You will use a **model** to help test your hypothesis.

Identify and control variables.

In the Big Dipper model used in this experiment, the **variable** that you change is the direction (front, side, above) from which you view the model. The variable you observe is how much the Big Dipper's appearance changes. The position of the "stars" is a variable you keep the same.

3ES4.a Students know the patterns of stars stay the same, although they appear to move across the sky nightly, and different stars can be seen in different seasons.
3IE5.a Repeat observations to improve accuracy and know that the results of similar scientific investigations seldom turn out exactly the same because of differences in the things being investigated, methods being used, or uncertainty in the observation. (Also **3IE5.0**)

Test your hypothesis.

1 Use the Pattern for a Big Dipper Model.
Label the straws from *A* to *G*.
Cut each to the correct length.

2 Make a foil ball around one end of each straw.

3 Put each straw on top of its letter on the
Pattern for the Big Dipper Model. Use a small
ball of clay to make each straw stand up.

Observe from the front, 2 steps back.
Identify the pattern you see.

Have a partner hold the Drawing
of the Big Dipper behind your model.
Do the stars line up?

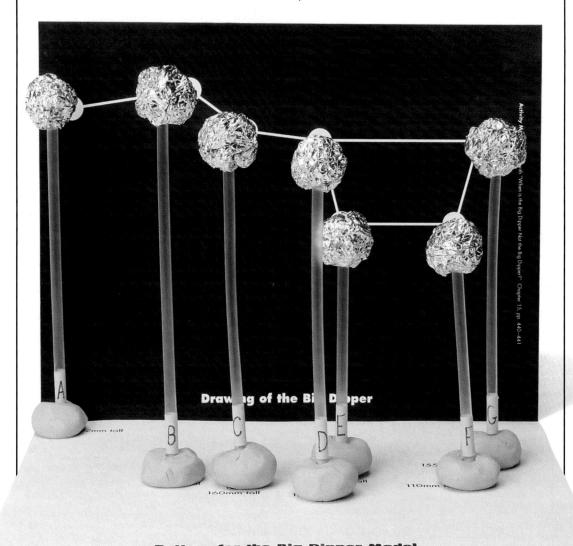

Drawing of the Big Dipper

Pattern for the Big Dipper Model

⑤ Make a drawing of the "stars" as seen
from the front, the left side, and above.

Collect and record your data.

Sketches or Drawings of Big Dipper Model		
View from Front	**View from Left Side**	**View from Above**

Interpret your data.

Compare the results of your investigation with those of another group. Are the results exactly the same? Explain.

State your conclusion.

Explain how the Big Dipper's appearance changes if observed from another part of the universe. Compare your hypothesis with your results. **Communicate** your conclusion.

Go Further

Do star patterns change as they "move" across the night sky? Can different ones be seen in different seasons? Find out.

...he Solar System

...a large sheet of paper and colored markers to make a model of the solar system. Label each planet. Include information about each planet and tell how long it takes to orbit the Sun.

Make a Moon Phase Book

Draw pictures showing the appearance of the Moon from Earth during the phases of the Moon. Be sure to label the phases. Make a book of your drawings.

Write a Fantasy

Write a fantasy about a trip through the solar system. Describe visiting three objects that are part of the solar system. Tell what you see, hear, and feel at each location. Remember that a fantasy is made up of events that could not happen in the real world.

Read More About Earth Sciences

Look for other books about earth sciences in your library. One book you may want to read is:

One Giant Leap: The Story of Neil Armstrong by Don Brown

Neil Armstrong was the first man to set foot on the Moon. In this book, Don Brown tells of Neil Armstrong's interest in air travel as a child. He also describes the astronaut's historic trip to the Moon.

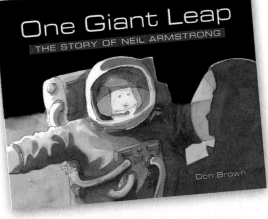

How do the sizes of planets compare?

Planets in the solar system differ in size.
Idea: Use a metric ruler and poster board to make models that compare the size of the Sun and each of the planets.

What factors affect the way a star looks?

Stars differ in brightness. Stars also differ in their distance from Earth.
Idea: Experiment with flashlights to test how the distance of a light source from the viewer affects its brightness. Use your results to make inferences about the brightness of stars.

What is the pattern of day length?

The Sun appears to rise in the east and set in the west. The number of hours the Sun appears in the sky changes from season to season.
Idea: Observe the time the Sun rises and sets every day for one month. Begin with a hypothesis. Keep accurate records with a watch and calendar. Use your data to show the pattern of daylight hours in your area.

Full Inquiry

Using Scientific Methods
1. Ask a question.
2. State a hypothesis.
3. Identify and control variables.
4. Test your hypothesis.
5. Collect and record your data.
6. Interpret your data.
7. State your conclusion.
8. Go further.

Unit C California Standards Practice

Write the letter of the correct answer.

1. **Which object moves across the sky against the fixed pattern of the stars?**
   A the Big Dipper
   B Saturn
   C the Sun
   D the North Star

2. **What is the path called that each planet takes as it revolves around the Sun?**
   A axis
   B orbit
   C phase
   D pole

3. **Which phase of the Moon is shown below?**

   A crescent Moon
   B Quarter Moon
   C New Moon
   D Full Moon

4. **The Moon completes one revolution around Earth once about every**
   A day.
   B week.
   C four weeks.
   D year.

5. **What do many telescopes have that make dim objects easier to see?**
   A They have machines that produce waves.
   B They have flashlights that shine light on the objects.
   C They have batteries that release stored energy.
   D They have mirrors that collect light.

6. What is the Sun?

   A The Sun is an asteroid.

   B The Sun is a constellation.

   C The Sun is a planet.

   D The Sun is a star.

7. Which of the following is a planet?

   A an asteroid

   B Orion

   C Neptune

   D the Moon

8. What affects the brightness of a star in the night sky?

   A stars surrounding it

   B distance of the star from Earth

   C motion of the star

   D position of the star in a constellation

9. In which position is Earth when it is winter in the southern half of Earth?

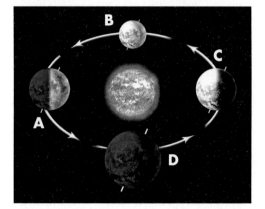

   A A

   B B

   C C

   D D

10. During which phase of the Moon is all of the Moon's lit part visible from Earth?

   A New Moon

   B First Quarter Moon

   C Third Quarter Moon

   D Full Moon

11. Why do stars seem to move across the sky at night?

A Earth rotates.

B The Moon rotates.

C Earth orbits the Sun.

D The Moon orbits Earth.

12. Stars in the northern sky appear to move in a circle around which object?

A the North Star

B the Moon

C Saturn

D the Little Dipper

13. Which part of the diagram shows the position of the Sun at noon?

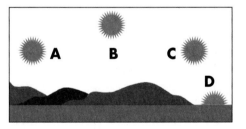

A A

B B

C C

D D

14. What happens to shadows as sunset approaches?

A They shorten.

B They stretch to the west.

C They disappear.

D They stretch to the east.

15. Why is the Moon visible in the sky?

A The Moon reflects light from the Sun.

B The Moon produces its own light.

C The Moon twinkles like a star.

D The Moon reflects light from nearby stars.

16. What does a telescope allow you to see?

A more stars than you can see with only your eyes

B details of planets outside the solar system

C the center of the Sun

D the other side of the Moon

17. What could you see if you viewed Mars through a telescope?

A thick clouds covering the planet

B red soil and white ice caps

C the Great Red Spot

D rings of rock and ice surrounding the planet

18. Which of the following shows the position of Earth when the northern half of Earth has the most hours of night?

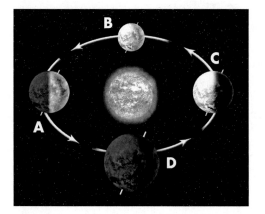

A A

B B

C C

D D

19. What causes different stars to appear in different seasons?

A Earth's rotation on its axis

B the lunar eclipse

C Earth's tilt as it orbits the Sun

D the phases of the Moon

20. What describes the stars in a constellation?

A The stars are the same distance from Earth.

B The stars are equally bright.

C The stars revolve around a planet.

D The stars form a pattern in the sky.

California Science Content Standards, Grade 3

STANDARD SET 1. Physical Sciences (Energy and Matter)

3PS1.0 Energy and matter have multiple forms and can be changed from one form to another. As a basis for understanding this concept:

3PS1.a Students know energy comes from the Sun to Earth in the form of light.	pp. 8, **9, 32, 34, 35,** 37, **45,** 104, 107, 119
3PS1.b Students know sources of stored energy take many forms, such as food, fuel, and batteries.	pp. **10, 11, 12, 13, 32,** 33, 34, 35, 88, 89, 99, 104, 107, 110
3PS1.c Students know machines and living things convert stored energy to motion and heat.	pp. 6, 12, 13, 14, **15, 17, 32,** 34, 35, 88, 100, 101, 102, 103, 107
3PS1.d Students know energy can be carried from one place to another by waves, such as water waves and sound waves, by electric current, and by moving objects.	pp. 2, **16, 18,** 19, **20,** 21, 22, 23, **24,** 25, 26, 27, 30, 31, **32,** 33, 34, 108
3PS1.e Students know matter has three forms: solid, liquid, and gas.	pp. **78, 79,** 80, **81,** 82, 83, **94, 96**
3PS1.f Students know evaporation and melting are changes that occur when the objects are heated.	pp. **80, 81,** 82, **83,** 95, **97,** 110
3PS1.g Students know that when two or more substances are combined, a new substance may be formed with properties that are different from those of the original materials.	pp. **84, 85, 86,** 87, 88, **92, 93,** 94, 110
3PS1.h Students know all matter is made of small particles called atoms, too small to see with the naked eye.	pp. 70, **74, 75,** 78, 79, **94,** 95, **96, 97,** 109
3PS1.i Students know people once thought that earth, wind, fire, and water were the basic elements that made up all matter. Science experiments show that there are more than 100 different types of atoms, which are presented on the periodic table of elements.	pp. **76, 77, 96, 97,** 109

What It Means to You

You can see the Sun's light and feel the Sun's heat all the time. You use stored food energy to move, grow, and stay warm. You can watch energy change matter. When you leave ice in a warm place, heat energy changes solid ice into a liquid. And if you leave the water there long enough, the water will turn into a gas.

EM1

California Science Content Standards, Grade 3

STANDARD SET 2. Physical Sciences (Light)

3PS2.0 Light has a source and travels in a direction. As a basis for understanding this concept:

3PS2.a Students know sunlight can be blocked to create shadows.	pp. 42, **45**, 46, 47, **62**, 63, 64, 65, **99**, 108
3PS2.b Students know light is reflected from mirrors and other surfaces.	pp. **50, 51**, 52, 53, 58, 59, 60, 61, **62**, 63, 64, 65, **99**, 108
3PS2.c Students know the color of light striking an object affects the way the object is seen.	pp. **54**, 55, 56, 57, **62**, 64, 65, **99**, 109
3PS2.d Students know an object is seen when light traveling from the object enters the eye.	pp. 45, **48**, 49, **62**, 64, 65, **99**, 108

What It Means to You

You see your face in a mirror and you see shadows because of the way light travels. Light is a form of energy. Light travels in a straight line from its source, so shadows form when objects block light. You see objects because light hits them, bounces off them, and then enters your eyes. Light bounces, or reflects, especially well from mirrors. Their shiny surface reflects the light rays so you can see your face. The color of an object depends on light that it reflects. An object's color also depends on the color of the light that hits it. For example, a box might appear white in white light, but it appears red under a red light.

California Science Content Standards, Grade 3

STANDARD SET 3. Life Sciences

3LS3.0 Adaptations in physical structure or behavior may improve an organism's chance for survival. As a basis for understanding this concept:

3LS3.a Students know plants and animals have structures that serve different functions in growth, survival, and reproduction.	pp. 116, 119, **120,** 121, 122, **123,** 125, **130,** 131, 133, 140, 141, 144, 145, 146, 148, 149, 185, 186, 187, 188, 189, 193, 194, 195
3LS3.b Students know examples of diverse life forms in different environments, such as oceans, deserts, tundra, forests, grasslands, and wetlands.	pp. **124,** 125, **126, 127, 128,** 129, 130, 132, 134, 135, 136, 137, 138, 139, **140, 141,** 146, 148, 149, 185, 190, 193
3LS3.c Students know living things cause changes in the environment in which they live: some of these changes are detrimental to the organism or other organisms, and some are beneficial.	pp. 157, **158,** 159, **160,** 161, 178, 180, 181, 185, 196
3LS3.d Students know when the environment changes, some plants and animals survive and reproduce; others die or move to new locations.	pp. 154, 157, 158, 160, **162, 163,** 165, 166, 167, 168, 176, 177, 178, 180, 181, 185, 194, 195, 196
3LS3.e Students know that some kinds of organisms that once lived on Earth have completely disappeared and that some of those resembled others that are alive today.	pp. **168,** 169, 170, 171, **172,** 173, 178, 180, 181, 184, 185, 193, 194

What It Means to You

Parts of your body help you live and grow. All plants and animals have body parts that help them live and grow in the places where they live. For example, desert cactuses have stems that can store water. Whales have a thick layer of blubber to keep them warm in cold ocean water. These adaptations help these living things survive in their environments. Plants and animals can change environments. Some plants and animals can still live in an environment that has changed. Others might die or move away. A kind of plant or animal that cannot adapt to a changed environment might become extinct.

California Science Content Standards, Grade 3

STANDARD SET 4. Earth Sciences

3ES4.0 Objects in the sky move in regular and predictable patterns. As a basis for understanding this concept:

3ES4.a Students know the patterns of stars stay the same, although they appear to move across the sky nightly, and different stars can be seen in different seasons.	pp. 205, 240, **242, 243, 244, 245,** 250, 252, 253, 255, 256, 257, 258, 259, 265, 266
3ES4.b Students know the way in which the Moon's appearance changes during the four-week lunar cycle.	pp. 240, **241,** 245, **248, 249,** 250, 252, 253, 255, 260, 263
3ES4.c Students know telescopes magnify the appearance of some distant objects in the sky, including the Moon and the planets. The number of stars that can be seen through telescopes is dramatically greater than the number that can be seen by the unaided eye.	pp. 198, **210,** 211, 212, 213, 214, 215, 218, 219, 220, 222, 223, 224, 225, 250, 254, 255, 263, 265
3ES4.d Students know that Earth is one of several planets that orbit the Sun and that the Moon orbits Earth.	pp. 202, 205, **206, 207, 208,** 209, 216, 217, 220, 240, 255, 260, 263, 264, 265
3ES4.e Students know the position of the Sun in the sky changes during the course of the day and from season to season.	pp. 230, 232, 233, **234, 235,** 236, 237, **238, 239,** 246, 247, 252, 253, 255, 264, 265, 266

What It Means to You

Sunlight in your window might wake you every morning. At night, it is dark outside. This pattern of day and night happens because Earth is spinning, or rotating, on its axis. At night, you see the Moon. Its shape changes in a regular pattern. Throughout a year, seasons also change in a regular pattern. This pattern happens because Earth's axis is tilted as Earth travels around the Sun. During this trip, different parts of Earth point more directly toward the Sun. Other planets orbit the Sun too. A telescope can help you see some of these planets and parts of the Moon more clearly. A telescope also helps you see many more stars than without a telescope.

California Science Content Standards, Grade 3

STANDARD SET 5. Investigation and Experimentation

3IE5.0 Scientific progress is made by asking meaningful questions and conducting careful investigations. As a basis for understanding this concept and addressing the content in the other three strands, students should develop their own questions and perform investigations. Students will:

3IE5.a Repeat observations to improve accuracy and know that the results of similar scientific investigations seldom turn out exactly the same because of differences in the things being investigated, methods being used, or uncertainty in the observation.	pp. **31,** 102, **103,** 116, **189, 230,** 259
3IE5.b Differentiate evidence from opinion and know that scientists do not rely on claims or conclusions unless they are backed by observations that can be confirmed.	pp. **70, 103, 254**
3IE5.c Use numerical data in describing and comparing objects, events, and measurements.	pp. **6,** 101, **102, 103, 145,** 176, **177, 202**
3IE5.d Predict the outcome of a simple investigation and compare the result with the prediction.	pp. **30, 31, 42, 219, 249**
3IE5.e Collect data in an investigation and analyze those data to develop a logical conclusion.	pp. **6,** 60, **61, 92, 93, 116, 154, 177, 189**

What It Means to You

What causes the appearance of the Moon to change? You can investigate and solve meaningful questions such as this one. The data you collect helps you draw conclusions about questions you ask. You measure things and use the numbers to compare them. For instance, you can measure a model of a cactus to see how it changes. You and a friend can observe the same thing, but draw different conclusions. Observations are different from opinions. For instance, your observations may show that a magazine picture is not solid but is made of small dots. You can then communicate with your friends the results of your investigation. When you make a model telescope, you can predict how objects far away will look. You can then compare your prediction with your observations.

Glossary

The glossary uses letters and signs to show how words are pronounced. The mark ′ is placed after a syllable with a primary or heavy accent. The mark ′ is placed after a syllable with a secondary or lighter accent.

To hear these words pronounced, listen to the AudioText CD.

absorb (ab sôrb′) take in something, such as light (p. 54)

adaptation (ad′ap tā′shən) a structure or ability that helps a plant or animal meet its needs (p. 120)

asteroid (as′tə roid′) a large piece of rock that orbits the Sun (p. 207)

atom (at′əm) the smallest particle of matter that has the properties of an element (p. 74)

axis (ak′sis) the imaginary line around which the Earth spins (p. 233)

balance (bal′əns) a tool for measuring mass (p. xviii)

binoculars (bə nok′yə lərz) two telescopes joined together as a unit (p. 211)

biome (bī′ōm) major areas that have a similar year-round weather pattern and support similar kinds of living things (p. 124)

camouflage (kam′ə fläzh) a color or pattern on an animal that makes it hard to see (p. 122)

chaparral (shap′ə ral′) a thick layer of evergreen shrubs, found in the southwestern United States (p. 124)

chemical change (kem′ ə kəl chānj) a change in which one kind of matter becomes a different kind of matter (p. 84)

classify (klas′ə fi ing) to arrange or sort objects, events, or living things according to their properties (p. xii)

collect data (kə lekt′ dā′tə) to gather observations and measurements into graphs, tables, charts, or labeled diagrams (p. xv)

color (kul′ ər) a property of an object determined by the light that reflects from the object (p. 54)

communicating (ke myü′nə kā ting) to use words, pictures, graphs, tables, charts, and labeled diagrams to share information (p. xv)

competition (kom′pə tish′ən) when two or more living things need the same resources (p. 157)

compression wave (kəm presh′ən wāv) a wave that carries energy by pushing particles together and then letting them spread apart (p. 20)

conclusion (kən klü′zhən) a decision or opinion based on evidence and reasoning (p. xvii)

coniferous forest (kō nif′ər əs fôr′ist) a forest of trees, most of which keep their leaves in winter (p. 134)

constellation (kon′stə lā′shən) a group of stars that make a fixed pattern (p. 242)

crater (krā′tər) a hole on a planet or moon made by something hitting it (p. 212)

crescent Moon (kres′nt mün) shape of the Moon when less than half of the Moon appears lit (p. 241)

cycle (sī′kəl) a repeating pattern of change over time (p. 160)

deciduous forest (di sij′ü əs əs fôr′ist) a forest of trees that lose all their leaves in the fall (p. 135)

desert (dez′ərt) an environment that gets very little rain (p. 130)

digestive system (de jes′tiv sis′təm) the system of body parts that helps animals break down the food they eat (p. 13)

direction (də rek′shn) a line along which something travels or can be seen (p. 45)

dry ice (drī īs) solid carbon dioxide (p. 81)

dwarf planet (dwôrf plan′it) small, round, ball-shaped object that revolves around the Sun (p. 207)

electricity (i let′tris′ə tē) electrical energy that moves through wires (p. 24)

element (el′ə mənt) matter made up of a single type of atom (p. 74)

energy (en′ər jē) the ability to do work or cause change; ability to make things move, stretch, or grow (p. 9)

energy of motion (en′ər jē ov mō′shen) the energy carried by moving objects (p. 14)

environment (en vī′rən mənt) everything that surrounds a living thing (p. 157)

estimate (es′tə māt) tell what you think an object's measurements are (p. xii)

evaporation (i vap′ə rā′ shen) when a liquid is changed into a gas (p. 80)

experiment (ek sper′ə mənt) to use scientific methods to test a hypothesis (p. xiv)

explore (ek splôr′) to study a scientific idea in a hands-on manner (p. xiv)

extinct (ek stingkt′) no longer lives on Earth (p. 168)

eye (ī) the part of the body that is sensitive to light energy (p. 48)

first quarter Moon (fėrst kwôr′ ter mün) phase of the Moon about a week after the new Moon when half the Moon appears lit (p. 241)

follow instructions (fol′ō in struk′shəns) to perform steps in the proper order that complete a task (p. 231)

forest (fôr′ist) an environment that has many trees (p. 134)

fossil (fos′əl) the remains or mark of a living thing from long ago (p. 168)

friction (frik′shən) when rubbing between objects changes energy of motion into heat energy (p. 17)

fuel (fyü′əl) something that can be burned to release stored energy that people can use (p. 12)

full Moon (fùl mün) phase of the Moon when all of the Moon appears lit (p. 241)

fungi (fung′jī) living things that can live inside dead matter, breaking it down and using it as food (p. 136)

fur (fėr) the covering of hair on some animals (p. 132)

galaxy (gal′ək sē) a group of stars, dust, and gas that are arranged together (p. 214)

gas (gas) matter that has no shape and has particles that are not held together (p. 79)

gills (gils) parts of fish that allow them to get the oxygen they need from water (p. 140, 141)

grassland (gras′land′) an environment that has many grasses and flowering plants, but few trees (p. 128)

growth (grōth) the process by which living things get bigger (p. 119)

habitat (hab′ə tat) the place where a living thing makes its home (p. 157)

heat (hēt) a form of energy that warms things (p. 17)

identify and control variables (ī den′tə fī and kən trōl vâr′ ē ə bəlz) to change one thing, but keep all the other factors the same (p. xvi)

infer (in fėr) draw a conclusion or make a reasonable guess based on what you have learned or what you know (p. xiii, 154)

interpret data (in tėr′prit dā′tə) to use the information you have collected to solve problems or answer questions (p. xv)

investigate (in ves′tə gāt) to solve a problem or answer a question by following an existing procedure or an original one (p. xiv)

lava (lä′və) the hot, liquid rock that erupts from a volcano (p. 82)

lens (lenz) a piece of glass shaped so it bends light a certain way (p. 210)

lichen (lī′kən) a living thing composed of a fungus and an algae that can survive in harsh environments (p. 133)

light (līt) a form of energy that travels in a straight line away from its source (p. 45)

lightning (līt′ning) the flash of light that occurs when electrical energy travels from the sky to the ground, often starting fires (p. 166)

liquid (lik′wid) matter that does not have a definite shape and is made of particles that are loosely held together (p. 78)

lungs (lungs) body parts in many animals that allow them to take in oxygen they need from the air (p. 141)

machine (mə shēn′) something that changes stored energy into motion and heat (p. 14)

main idea and details (mān ī dē′ ə and di tālz′), a primary concept and the facts that support it (p. 7, p. 117)

make inferences (māk in′fər ən əz) to use data to develop a logical conclusion (p. 155)

matter (mat′ər) anything that has mass and takes up space (p. 73)

measure (mezh′ər) to use a tool to find the size or amount of something (p. xii)

melting (melting) changing from a solid to a liquid (p. 81)

mirror (mir′ər) a surface made of shiny material (p. 51)

mixture (miks′chər) two or more types of matter together, but which can easily be separated (p. 86)

model (mod′l) a sketch, diagram, or object that represents something else (p. xiii)

Moon (mün) the large sphere that orbits Earth (p. 208)

motion (mō′shən) a change in the position of an object (p. 14)

new Moon (nü mün) phase of the Moon when none of the Moon appears lit (p. 241)

nuclear energy (nü′klē ər en′ər jē) a form of energy from special fuel used to produce heat that is changed into electricity (p. 26)

nutrients (nü′trē əntz) small particles in food, soil and air that plants and animals need to grow (p. 119)

object (ob′jikt) a thing or piece of matter (p. 16, 50)

observe (əb zèrv′) to use your senses to find out about objects, events, or living things (p. xii)

ocean (ō′shən) salt water that covers much of the Earth's surface (p. 140)

opaque (ō pāk′) describes materials that block light (p. 46)

orbit (ôr′ bit) the path an object takes as it moves around the Sun (p. 206)

periodic table (pir′ē od′ik tā′bəl) a chart with elements arranged in rows and columns according to their properties (p. 77)

phases of the Moon (fāz əz′ ov ᴛʜə mün) set of each of the different ways that the Moon looks (p. 241)

planet (plan′it) a large, round, ball-shaped body of matter that revolves around a star such as the Sun (p. 206)

predict (pri dikt′) to tell what you think will happen (p. 43, 203)

property (prop′ər tē) something about matter that can be observed with one or more senses (p. 73)

reflect (ri flekt′) bounce off, as a light wave does from an object (p. 50)

reproduction (rē′prə duk′shən) the process by which living things produce offspring (p. 119)

resource (ri′sôrs) any supply that will meet a need (p. 157)

revolution (rev′ə lü′shən) one complete trip an object takes around another object (p. 236)

rotation (rō tā′shən) one complete spin on an axis (p. 234)

scientific method (sā′ən tif′ik meth′əd) organized ways of finding answers and solving problems (p. xvi)

sequence (sē′kwəns) the order in which events take place (p. 71)

shadow (shad′ō) an area that does not receive light directly (p. 46)

shelter (shel′tər) place animals use for protection from the weather and other animals (p. 119)

solar system (sō′lər sis′təm) a system made up of the Sun, the planets and their moons, and other objects that orbit the Sun (p. 206)

solid (sol′id) matter that has a definite shape and is made of particles that are firmly held together (p. 78)

sound (sound) a form of energy produced when things vibrate, which you can hear (p. 20)

space probe (spās prōb) a vehicle that carries cameras and other tools for studying distant objects in space (p. 213)

star (stär) a huge ball of hot, glowing gases (p. 205)

stored energy (stôrd en′ər jē) energy that can be changed into a form that can do work (p. 10)

substance (sub′stəns) any amount of matter (p. 73)

Sun (sun) the star closest to Earth that gives off light (p. 205)

surface (sėr′fis) the outside of an object (p. 50)

survival (sər vī′vəl) continuing to live (p. 119)

symbol (sim′bəl) a letter or drawing that represents something else (p. 77)

telescope (tel′ə skōp) a tool for making distant objects appear nearer and larger (p. 210)

third quarter Moon (thėrd kwôr′ter mün) phase of the Moon about three weeks after the new Moon when half the Moon appears lit (p. 241)

tundra (tən′ drə) a cold, dry environment located in the most northern part of the world and on high mountains (p. 132)

variable (vâr′ē bəl) a thing or a quality that is subject to change (p. xiv)

vibrate (vī′ brāt) move back and forth (p. 20)

waning Moon (wān′ ing mün) when less of the lit half of the Moon appears each night (p. 241)

water vapor (wȯ′tər vā′ pər) water in the form of a gas (p. 80)

wave (wāv) a repeating movement in matter that moves energy from one place to another (p. 18)

waxing Moon (waks′ ing mün) when more of the lit half of the Moon appears each night (p. 241)

wetland (wet′land′) a low area that is covered by water at least part of the year (p. 138)

Index

This index lists the pages on which topics appear in this book. Page numbers after a *p* refer to a photograph or drawing. Page numbers after a *c* refer to a chart, graph, or diagram.

189

Credits

Illustrations

11, 13, 24 Tony Randazzo; 21 Jeff Mangiat; 28, 142, 200, 206, 208, 228-229, 234, 236-237, 239, 241, 250, 264, 266 Paul Oglesby; 35, 65, 97, 107-108, 110, 149, 181, 193-196, 223, 253, 263, 265 Luciana Navarro Powell; 40, 48-49, 231-232, 236, 250, 264 Robert Kayganich; 78-79, 81, 228 Big Sesh Studios; 126 Robert Ulrich; 130, 170 Alan Barnard; 153, 168, 172, 250 Peter Bollinger; 205 Studio Liddell

Photographs

Every effort has been made to secure permission and provide appropriate credit for photographic material. The publisher deeply regrets any omission and pledges to correct errors called to its attention in subsequent editions.

Unless otherwise acknowledged, all photographs are the property of Scott Foresman, a division of Pearson Education.

Photo locators denoted as follows: Top (T), Center (C), Bottom (B), Left (L), Right (R), Background (Bkgd).

Cover: (L) ©Michele Westmorland/ Corbis, (C) ©Martin Harvey/Corbis

Front Matter:

iii (BR) ©Daniel J. Cox/Natural Exposures, (TR) Getty Images; v ©Frans Lanting/Minden Pictures; vi (TL) ©Spencer Rowell/Getty Images, (BL) ©Altrendo Travel/Getty Images; vii (TR) Getty Images, (BR) ©Neal Mishler/Getty Images; viii (TL) ©Phil Schermeister/Getty Images, (B) ©Vittoriano Rastelli/Corbis; ix ©Klaus Nigge/Getty Images; x (TL) ©Earth Imaging/Getty Images, (BR) Andy Crawford/©DK Images; xi ©Ian McKinnell/Getty Images; xii Demetrio Carrasco/©DK Images; xiii ©Amadej Trnkoczy; xiv ©Claver Carroll/Photo Library; xv Dr. Lloyd Glenn Ingles/©California Academy of Sciences

Unit A – Opener: 1 (Bkgd) ©Henrik Sorensen/Getty Images, (C) Getty Images; 2 Getty Images; 3 ©Spencer Rowell/Getty Images; 4 (T) ©O. Eckstein/Corbis, (BR) ©Tom Benoit/SuperStock; 5 (TR) ©Gary Rhijnsburger/Masterfile Corporation, (B) ©Richard Pasley/Stock Boston; 7 (CR) ©Royalty-Free/Corbis, (Bkgd) ©O. Eckstein/Corbis; 8 ©O. Eckstein/Corbis; 9 ©Jim Steinberg/Photo Researchers, Inc.; 10 (TL) Getty Images, (TR) ©Doug Wilson/Alamy Images; 12 (TL) Rubberball Productions, (CL) ©Dan and Coco McCoy/Rainbow; 13 Getty Images; 14 (TL) ©G. Bell/Corbis, (CL) ©Tom Benoit/SuperStock, (BL) AGE Fotostock; 15 (TL) ©AGStockUSA, Inc./Alamy Images, (TCL) ©Henryk T. Kaiser/Index Stock Imagery, (CL) ©Lester Lefkowitz/Corbis, (BCL) ©Mark L. Stephenson/Corbis, (BL) ©Mark C. Burnett/Photo Researchers, Inc.; 16 ©Tim Ridley/©DK Images; 17 ©Richard Pasley/Stock Boston; 18 (CL) ©Ted Grant/Masterfile Corporation, (L) ©Tom Szuba/ Masterfile Corporation; 20 (TL, L) Getty Images; 22 (B, TL) ©Lloyd Cluff/Corbis; 23 (TR) ©Ken M. John/ Photo Researchers, Inc., (CR) ©Spencer Grant/Photo Researchers, Inc.; 25 ©Gary Rhijnsburger/ Masterfile Corporation; 26 (TL, B) ©Bettmann/Corbis; 27 (BC) Getty Images, (T) ©E. R. Degginger/Color-Pic, Inc., (TC) ©Larry Lee Photography/Corbis, (B) ©Jim Wark/ Peter Arnold, Inc.; 28 ©Tony McConnell/Photo Researchers, Inc.; 29 (TR) ©B. A. E. Inc./Alamy Images, (CR) ©Heather Angel/ Natural Visions; 32 (Bkgd) ©Stockbyte/Getty Images, (TL) ©Tom Benoit/SuperStock, (CL) ©Ted Grant/ Masterfile Corporation, (BL) ©Larry Lee Photography/Corbis, (BR) ©Richard Pasley/Stock Boston, (TL) ©O. Eckstein/Corbis; 34 ©Tim Ridley/©DK Images; 36 (Bkgd) ©Craig Aurness/Corbis, (B) ©Mark Edwards/Peter Arnold, Inc.; 37 Corbis; 38 (BR) NASA, (Bkgd) Jupiter Images; 39 ©Altrendo Travel/Getty Images; 40 (BL) ©Royalty-Free/ Corbis, (T) ©Craig Tuttle/Corbis; 41 (BR) ©Steve Gorton/©DK Images, (BL) ©Daryl Benson/Masterfile Corporation; 43 ©Craig Tuttle/ Corbis; 44 ©Craig Tuttle/Corbis; 45 ©Joseph Baylor Roberts/NGS Image Collection; 46 ©Royalty-Free/Corbis; 47 (TR) ©Pierre Arsenault/Masterfile Corporation, (L) ©Royalty-Free/ Corbis; 50 ©Daryl Benson/ Masterfile Corporation; 54 ©Steve Gorton/©DK Images; 62 (BR) ©DK Images, (Bkgd) ©Masao Kurosawa/ Getty Images, (B) ©Craig Tuttle/ Corbis, (CL) ©Daryl Benson/ Masterfile Corporation; 64 ©Steve Gorton/©DK Images; 66 (B, Bkgd) ©Royalty-Free/Corbis; 67 Getty Images; 68 ©Tony Freeman/ PhotoEdit; 69 PhotoLibrary; 71 (Bkgd) ©Tony Freeman/PhotoEdit, (BL) ©Sinclair Stammers/Photo Researchers, Inc.; 72 ©Tony Freeman/PhotoEdit; 73 ©Brand X Pictures/Getty Images; 76 (BL) Mary Evans Picture Library, (B) Michael Hughes/©Aurora Photos; 77 ©Neal Mishler/Getty Images; 78 (TL) Stephen Oliver/©DK Images, (BR) ©DK Images; 80 (TL) Getty Images, (BL) ©Brand X Pictures/Getty Images; 81 ©Charles D. Winters/Photo Researchers, Inc.; 82 (TL) ©Jim Sugar/Corbis, (R) ©Robert Madden/ NGS Image Collection, (BC) Digital Vision; 83 (L) ©William Taufic/ Corbis, (TC) Matthew Ward/©DK Images; 84 (TCL) Jupiter Images, (TL) Dave King/Pitt Rivers Museum/ University of Oxford/©DK Images; 85 (BR, B) ©DK Images, (TR) ©Richard Megna/Fundamental Photographs; 86 ©DK Images; 87 ©DK Images; 88 (BC) ©Stone/Getty Images, (TL) ©Brand X Pictures/Getty Images; 89 (TR) PhotoLibrary, (B) ©Doug Scott/AGE Fotostock; 94 (Bkgd) Getty Images, (TL) ©Tony Freeman/PhotoEdit, (BL) ©Richard Megna/Fundamental Photographs; 98 (BR, L) Courtesy of Dr. John Pojman, (Bkgd) Getty Images; 99 (TL) ©Spencer Rowell/Getty Images, (CL) ©Altrendo Travel/Getty Images, (BL, BR) Getty Images; 104 (T) ©Jens Lucking/Getty Images, (B) Andy Crawford/©DK Images; 105 ©Michael Dalton/Fundamental Photographs; 106 ©Alan Kearney/ Getty Images; Unit B – Opener: 111 (BR) ©Michael Nichols/Getty Images, (Bkgd) ©Gail Shumway/ Getty Images; 112 ©Ruth Tomlinson/ Getty Images; 113 (Bkgd) ©Phil Schermeister/Getty Images, (CR) ©Roger Archibald/Animals Animals/ Earth Scenes; 114 (BR) ©J. Eastcott/ Y. Eastcott Film/NGS Image Collection, (BL) ©Enzo & Paolo Ragazzini/Corbis, (T) ©Tom Brakefield/Corbis; 115 (BR) ©Charles Schafer/SuperStock, (BL) ©Andy Binns/Ecoscene, (C) ©Daniel J. Cox/Natural Exposures, (R) ©Ken Lucas/Visuals Unlimited; 117 ©Tom Brakefield/Corbis; 118 ©Tom Brakefield/Corbis; 119 ©The Image Bank/Getty Images; 120 (TR) ©Ken Lucas/Visuals Unlimited, (TL) ©Tony Evans/Timelapse Library/Getty Images, (B) ©DK Images; 121 (TC) ©Frans Lanting/Minden Pictures, (TR) ©Kevin Schafer/Corbis, (CR) ©Gary W. Carter/Corbis, (BR) ©DK Images; 122 (TL) ©James Robinson/Animals Animals/Earth Scenes, (BR) ©Vittoriano Rastelli/Corbis; 123 (TL) ©Michael Quinton/Minden Pictures, (C) ©The Image Bank/Getty Images, (BL) ©Rolf Kopfle/Bruce Coleman Inc., (BR) ©Rick & Nora Bowers/ Visuals Unlimited, (TCL) ©Rod Planck/Photo Researchers, Inc., (BCL) ©Tim Laman/NGS Image Collection, (TCR) ©Ken Wilson/Papilio/Corbis, (TR) ©Chris Newbert/Minden Pictures, (CR) ©Steve E. Ross/Photo Researchers, Inc., (CR) ©David Aubrey/Corbis, (BCR) ©Suzanne L. & Joseph T. Collins/Photo Researchers, Inc., (BR) ©E. R. Degginger/Bruce Coleman Inc., (TR) Neil Fletcher/©DK Images; 124 (CR) ©Royalty-Free/ Corbis, (TL) ©Peter Chadwick/©DK Images, (R) ©Ken Lucas/Visuals Unlimited, (TR) ©W. Perry Conway/ Corbis; 125 ©John Cancalosi/ Nature Picture Library; 126 (BL) ©Andrew Brown/Ecoscene/Corbis, (TL) ©W. Wayne Lockwood, M.D./